Online Security
for the
Older Generation

Jim Gatenby

BERNARD BABANI (publishing) LTD
The Grampians
Shepherds Bush Road
London W6 7NF
England

www.babanibooks.com

Please Note

Although every care has been taken with the production of this book to ensure that all information is correct at the time of writing and that any projects, designs, modifications and/or programs, etc., contained herewith, operate in a correct and safe manner and also that any components specified are normally available in Great Britain, the Publishers and Author do not accept responsibility in any way for the failure (including fault in design) of any project, design, modification or program to work correctly or to cause damage to any equipment that it may be connected to or used in conjunction with, or in respect of any other damage or injury that may be so caused, nor do the Publishers accept responsibility in any way for the failure to obtain specified components.

Notice is also given that if equipment that is still under warranty is modified in any way or used or connected with home-built equipment then that warranty may be void.

© 2018 BERNARD BABANI (publishing) LTD

First Published – October 2018

British Library Cataloguing in Publication Data:

A catalogue record for this book is available from the British Library

ISBN 978-0-85934-775-4

Cover Design by Gregor Arthur

Printed and bound in Great Britain for Bernard Babani (publishing) Ltd

About this Book

Many of us now use computers for some of the most important tasks in our lives, such as online banking and shopping. Or keeping in touch with friends and family using e-mail and social networking with Facebook and Twitter, etc.

Unfortunately these very activities can leave us wide open to attack by fraudsters wishing to steal our money and private information. If you lead a busy life or are not too experienced with smartphones, tablets and other computers, it's easy to fall for a scam from one of the new breed of very clever cyber criminals. Even with many years of teaching and working with computers, I fell for an e-mail "phishing" scam which took money from my bank account.

However, it's not all bad news. There are many steps you can take to hang on to your money and protect your private data. The first few chapters explain the various types of crime and malicious software. Browsing the Internet safely is covered, followed by checking the security settings on your device. Later chapters discuss software you can install to protect your computer and how to use free public Wi-Fi networks safely.

It's very easy to lose important data stored on your device, either through cyber crime or accidentally. Chapter 12 describes how to make backup copies of valuable photos, documents and data files, saved either in the "Clouds" on the Internet or on separate storage media such as USB drives. So it's easy for anyone to make sure their data is safe. In fact it's so easy that, in using computers to produce nearly 60 books like this one, I can honestly claim never to have lost as much as a single paragraph.

About the Author

Jim Gatenby trained as a Chartered Mechanical Engineer and initially worked at Rolls-Royce Ltd using computers in the analysis of jet engine performance. He obtained a Master of Philosophy degree in Mathematical Education by research at Loughborough University of Technology and taught mathematics and computing in school for many years before becoming a full-time author. The author has written over fifty books in the fields of educational computing, Android tablets and smartphones and Microsoft Windows, including many of the titles in the highly successful "Older Generation" series from Bernard Babani (publishing) Ltd, all of which have been very well received.

Trademarks

Android, Google, Google Drive and Chrome, are trademarks or registered trademarks of Google, Inc. Microsoft Windows, Microsoft Edge and Internet Explorer are trademarks or registered trademarks of Microsoft Corporation. iPhone, iPad, iCloud, iCloud Drive, iOS and Safari are trademarks or registered trademarks of Apple Inc. Kaspersky Internet Security is a trademark of Kaspersky Lab. Firefox is a trademark of the Mozilla Foundation. Norton Security is a trademark of Symantec Corporation. AVG Anti-Virus is a trademark or registered trademark of AVG Technologies. All other brand and product names used in this book are recognized as trademarks or registered trademarks, of their respective companies.

Acknowledgements

I would like to thank my wife Jill for her support during the preparation of this book and also Michael Babani for making the project possible.

Contents

What is There to Fear?

The Scam

According to the Oxford English Dictionary, a *scam* is a trick, a swindle or a fraud. The Internet is the perfect arena for scammers and fraudsters to ply their criminal trade.

I Should Have Known Better

Having used computers for more years than I care to remember, I should have known better than to fall for the following scam:

An innocent looking e-mail arrived, apparently from a company we'd previously ordered goods from. It included a *link* shown in blue below:

"**More information about your order available here**"

The company details and layout of the e-mail were exactly the same as previous messages and so I naively clicked on the link. This led to my computer being invaded by a *Trojan Horse*, a small malicious program or piece of code that can give fraudsters access to your data. The result was £632 taken from our bank account.

The bank covered the loss in this scam, but this may not always be the case now we are more aware of scams.

Scams like the above cost UK computer users billions of pounds — in some cases their life savings. However, by taking suitable precautions (like not clicking on links to Web sites in an e-mail or text message as I did), it's possible to beat the fraudsters and stay safe online.

The next few pages outline some common scams or computer crimes. Subsequent chapters describe ways to make your computing activities as safe as possible.

Your Digital Footprint

Most of this book will discuss the possible threats to your finances and private information as a result of having a *digital footprint*. This is the trail of data you leave behind after going online to the Internet to visit websites and send e-mails, etc. The data you put on the Internet deliberately such as e-mails and your personal details when buying goods online, etc., is known as your *active digital footprint*. Data about you is also collected automatically, without your knowledge and is known as your *passive digital footprint*. This would include a list of the Web sites you've visited.

Cyber Crime

Obviously the greater your digital footprint the greater the need to protect your personal data and finances from online crime and fraud, also known as *cyber crime*.

All computers can be affected, including smartphones.

Nowadays many people of all ages use computers in one form or another — smartphone, tablet, laptop or desktop. Despite its small size, the smartphone is a fully fledged, powerful computer. The huge popularity of the smartphone and its use for a vast range of Internet activities such as online banking and shopping has also increased the opportunities for cyber crime.

Throughout this book, unless otherwise stated, *computer* refers to smartphones, tablets, laptops and desktop machines, which may all be subjected to cyber crime.

Examples of Cyber Crime

As mentioned earlier some people have been scammed out of their life savings, with losses of £50,000 or more being not unusual. Many scams, (like the one I succumbed to) arrive in an unsolicited e-mail or text message. Some examples of scams include:

An Online "Friend" Desperately Needs Cash

Scammers often target people who are vulnerable or lonely. A fraudster befriends someone online over a period of time and, having gained their trust, starts asking for money to overcome heartrending personal or financial problems. This might happen on a social network or on a dating website.

"You've Won a Prize"

A person is told they've won a cash prize or inherited some money and need to enter their bank account details in a website in order to receive the payment.

Nigeria 419 Scam

Many scammers operate from overseas. This scam started in Nigeria where it was listed as 419 in the Criminal Code. Now prevalent around the world, the scam asks for help to transfer money "trapped" in Nigeria or elsewhere, perhaps due to a conflict. You are offered a generous payment or a share of the funds to transfer the money out of the country via your bank account. You may also be asked to make payments to cover the transfer fees. After giving your bank account details, no money is transferred to you but your account is drained of funds.

HMRC Refund Scam

The scammers send an official-looking e-mail asking for your bank details so they can refund tax you have overpaid.

"I'm stranded abroad with no money"

Several people receive an e-mail, apparently from a friend, asking for cash or your bank account details to allow them to return home. .

"Your account is no longer safe"

An e-mail, apparently from your bank, says that there is a problem with your account. You are asked to click or tap a link and verify your account details.

"Regarding your recent order"

You receive an e-mail, apparently from a company you've previously ordered goods from. It asks you to click or tap a link to check your latest (phoney) order. This leads to a *Trojan Horse* taking control of your computer and getting access to your bank account.

"Our bank account details have changed"

Someone pretending to be working for a solicitor or other firm to whom you need to make large payments, asks you to make future payments to their new account. The scammer then gives you details of his or her own account.

Identity Theft

This is a crime in which people steal your personal details and pretend to be you. This might involve using your name, etc., to take out loans, obtain a passport, commit crimes, send out e-mails or posts on social media to embarrass you or damage your reputation.

Fake Computer Games

You buy what you think is a genuine copy of a top-selling game. The game is a fake and contains spyware, designed to steal your data and damage your computer.

Online Shopping Fraud

This often involves fake Web sites advertising goods which never arrive.

"There are problems with your computer"

You receive an e-mail or phone call, falsely claiming to be from Microsoft. The caller says there are problems with your computer and you must pay to fix them. They then install *spyware* allowing them to see everything you do on your computer.

Or you receive an e-mail saying "You need to confirm your Office 365 details." Microsoft state that they don't send out unsolicited e-mails or make phone calls asking for personal information or offering to fix computers.

Cyber Bullying

This is the use of social networks, e-mails and messages to embarrass and humiliate other people using adverse comments, criticism and false information. This is all too easy now with the widespread use of smartphones.

Although there is not a UK law covering cyber bullying itself, the bully may be charged with crimes such as using threatening behaviour, harassment or causing anxiety.

With children this can lead to depression and lack of confidence. Millions of older people spend many hours a week looking after grandchildren and need to be aware of the dangers of online bullying amongst children.

Adults may also be victims of cyber bullying, resulting in damage to their health, career, business or reputation. Many people in the UK take time off work due to illness caused by *workplace cyber bullying*.

Some Relevant Jargon

Hacker

A computer expert who may work legally to test the security of systems or, in some cases, to access a computer to steal personal information or to cause problems.

Phishing

This means "fishing" for your personal information such as name, address, bank account details, passwords, often via an e-mail which includes a link to a fraudulent website. The message then asks you to update your personal details.

Smishing

This term, also written as SMiShing, is phishing using an SMS (Short Message Service) text message.

Software

Programs or *code* written in a special programming language, consisting of *statements* or instructions for a computer to execute.

Malware

An umbrella term covering various types of *malicious software*, designed to cause damage and inconvenience. Writing and distributing malware is a criminal offence which may result in a prison sentence.

Various types of malware are discussd briefly on the next page and in more detail in Chapter 11.

Chapter 11 also discusses installing and using third-party software designed to protect your computer, tablet or smartphone from malware.

Worms

A worm is a program that repeatedly copies itself onto the hard disk or Internal Storage of your computer. This fills up your storage and slows down your computer.

Viruses

These are small, malicious programs intended to delete data, steal information and send out spam e-mails, etc. A virus may be attached to an e-mail or in files downloaded from the Internet and may spread to other computers.

Trojans

The Trojan Horse, like its namesake, is a program which appears to be genuine but is designed to gain access to your computer and your personal information.

Adware

These are advertising banners which pop up when you are running a program or viewing a website. They may be used to gather information about you for marketing purposes.

Spyware

This is similar to adware but is installed covertly when you install other software on your computer. Spyware can access your personal information and track your browsing activities, perhaps for marketing purposes.

Cookies

A cookie is not malware but a small text file which stores information about you and your Web browsing activities. Cookies are discussed in more detail in Chapter 3.

Eliminating the Dangers

There are lots of steps you can take to protect your computer from attack, whether it's a smartphone, tablet, laptop or desktop computer. These include optimising your device's inbuilt security settings and installing third party anti-virus and Internet Security software. These practical safeguards are discussed in the rest of this book. In the meantime, there are some simple precautions that can reduce the risk of trouble, such as:

- Don't click or tap on links in e-mails or text messages.
- Don't enter your bank account details unless you are sure of the organisation or business requesting them.
- Check requests for your bank details by phoning a number you know to be genuine or contact the bank, organisation or individual in writing or in person.
- Look for spelling mistakes and errors in e-mails, text messages Web pages appearing to be from banks, etc.
- Banks don't ask you to enter your full password — only selected letters or digits, e.g. second and fifth.
- Be wary of offers to invest your savings or pension in new ventures — if they fail you may lose everything.
- Important data files or photos could be deleted by viruses, or you might delete them accidentally.
- Important files should be stored in the *clouds* on the Internet so they can be accessed on any computer.
- Back up copies should be made on removable media such as a CD, memory stick/flash drive or an external disk drive.

What is the Internet?

Introduction

The Internet is certainly the most important technological development in the world in the last 20 or 30 years. Also known as the Net, the World Wide Web and, in previous years, the Information Superhighway, it is now the main form of communication between people around the world, for both work and leisure. As discussed throughout this book, there are many other applications of the Internet, apart from its original use for exchanging text messages.

Another phase in the evolution of the Internet is "The Internet of Things", where "Things" refers to a wide range of machines, vehicles, domestic appliances and robots. These devices can be connected to the Internet and monitored and controlled from anywhere in the world. One example of this technology being applied is a surgeon operating on a patient hundreds of miles away, in another country. The surgeon sends instructions over the Internet to control a robot which actually carries out the operation.

However, most of us will use the Internet for everyday tasks like online banking and shopping, communicating with friends using e-mail and social networking, promoting a small business or finding news and information. Though perhaps not as exciting as controlling a robot hundreds of miles away, these everyday activities are not without risks which can lead to serious financial losses, theft of personal data and invasion of privacy, as discussed in Chapter 1.

Components of the Internet

The Internet is a ***network of networks***, like spiders' webs connecting computers around the world. The computers are connected by Wi-Fi (wireless technology), telephone landlines, cell phone masts and networks and satellites.

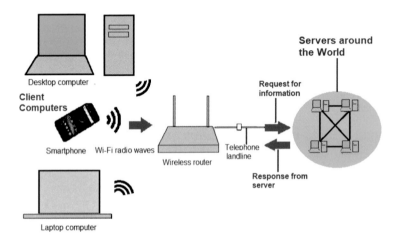

There are two main categories of computer connected to the Internet, known as ***Web servers*** and ***Web clients***.

Web Servers

These are computers storing the information and services which users can access. Information created by an organisation or individual is stored on the server as a *website* consisting of one or more ***Web pages***.

There are millions of Web servers situated around the world, many of them operated by large companies such as Microsoft, Google and Facebook.

Small organisations and individuals can also set up a computer to act as a server to allow other people to access information on their computer.

The *Clouds* refers to the use of Web servers for the storage of data rather than locally on your hard disk drive, etc.

We can use Web servers to store our data in the *Clouds*, using storage systems such as OneDrive, Google Drive and Dropbox. This frees up space on our local Internal Storage such as a hard disk drive or an SSD (Solid State Drive). Cloud storage also provides a secure *backup system* accessible on any computer connected to the Internet.

Web Clients

These are the computers we use to connect to the Internet and access information from Web servers, which may be anywhere in the world. Originally many people used desktop computers, but then laptops and tablets became popular devices for going *online* to the "Net".

In recent years the smartphone has emerged as a powerful computer as well as a mobile phone. With its relatively low price and excellent portability, the smartphone is the favourite device for many people to use for most, if not all, of their Internet activities.

IP Address

The IP (Internet Protocol) Address is a unique number to identify client computers, servers and other devices on the Internet, similar to the address of a house. Your IP address is needed so that a Web server can return information to your computer. A typical IP address is shown below:

151.168. 1.121

Connecting to the Internet Using Wi-Fi

Wi-Fi is the most common method of connecting to the Internet in the home or office, using a device called a *wireless router*. The router is a box into which a cable can be attached to connect the router to the Internet via a telephone landline. Several client computers in the home or office can be connected wirelessly to the router, forming a *home* or *local area network*.

Wi-Fi Router

Modern computers such as smartphones, tablets, laptops and desktops have the necessary Wi-Fi technology built in to connect wirelessly to the router. Otherwise, for older computers, you can buy *network adapters* to make a wireless connection.

Internet Service Providers (ISPs)

An ISP is a company such as BT, Sky, Virgin Media and TalkTalk that enables you to connect to the Internet via their network. Many supply a Wi-Fi router as part of a 12 or 18 month contract for which you pay a monthly fee, of perhaps £20-£40.

Most ISPs use the BT telephone landlines for connecting to the Internet. 90% of homes in the UK now have access to the latest high speed *broadband* Internet delivered over *fibre optic* telephone cables rather than *copper cables*.

Your Internet Service Provider allocates the IP address of your computer.

The Need for a Wi-Fi Password

When setting up a Wi-Fi router you will need to enter a *password* or *wireless key* provided by your ISP. This is necessary because anyone with a smartphone, tablet, laptop etc., within the range of your router (typically 300 feet or 92 metres outdoors) can detect your router and home network.

This includes any of your neighbours within range or anyone outside, perhaps in a car. Apart from using the network you pay for, they may also be hacking or carrying out illegal activities. You might be blamed for any offences, since these would be traceable to you through your computer's IP address (discussed on page 11).

The solution is to set a very strong and unguessable password for your router.

Public Wi-Fi

If you are using a smartphone, tablet or laptop away from home or your office, etc., there are many public Wi-Fi Internet access points, in cafes, airports, hotels, etc. Many of them are free and do not require a password. These should not be used for sending or receiving private information over the Internet.

Free public Wi-Fi may be easily attacked by hackers.

13

Connecting Using a Cell Phone Network

As well as using a Wi-Fi router, smartphones (and some tablet computers) can also connect to the Internet using a *cell phone network*, such as EE, O2, Gigaff, Tesco Mobile and Three. This connection is known as *mobile data*.

The advantage of using a phone network is that you can connect to the Internet in places where there is no Wi-Fi. Your smartphone (and certain tablets) connect wirelessly to the masts of the cell phone network and then on to the Internet using the public telephone network and satellites. Cell phone networks are currently known as 3G/4G (3rd and 4th Generation) with 5G currently being developed.

Wi-Fi versus Mobile Data

It's cheaper to use a Wi-Fi router where available, rather than the cell phone network. This is because mobile phone contracts generally have a limit on the amount of Internet data you can *download*, i.e. copy to your computer. Most Wi-Fi contracts allow unlimited free data. Using mobile data abroad can lead to unexpectedly large bills and should be avoided where possible.

Using a Smartphone as a Mobile Hotspot

In places where there is no Wi-Fi, a smartphone can be used like a *router*. The smartphone is connected to the Internet using mobile data as discussed above. Several other devices such as Wi-Fi only tablets and laptops can be connected to the smartphone by their Wi-Fi, or a *Bluetooth connection* or a cable, in a process known as *tethering*. The smartphone then shares its Internet connection with the tethered devices.

A mobile hotspot is more secure than public Wi-Fi.

Software

So far this chapter has mainly discussd the *hardware* which makes up the Internet — the physical devices and components such as client and server computers, telephone landlines, cell phone masts or towers and satellites.

The hardware has to be controlled by sets of instructions or *programs* written by people using one of many special programming languages. There are many types of program for different purposes and these are collectively known as *software*. As discussed in detail elsewhere in this book, there are also programs written for malicious purposes such as obtaining personal information, stealing money or damaging your computer. Software written with criminal intent is known by the umbrella title of *malware*.

System Software

This consists of programs written to control all of the basic functions of a computer, no matter what you are using it for. This includes running or executing programs, controlling the screen display, printing and connecting to the Internet. The *Operating System* (OS) contains most of the system software. The operating system is pre-installed on a new computer, permanently saved on the Internal Storage such as a hard disc drive or SSD . Well-known operating systems are Windows, Android, iOS and macOS.

As discussed in Chapters 8-10, the operating system contains many security features to protect your computer from *hackers*, i.e. fraudsters. These are updated regularly by "patches" or security improvements, *downloaded* from the Internet and saved on your computer's Internal Storage.

Always keep your operating system up-to-date.

15

Applications Software

This is the software needed to carry out a particular task, which you personally want to do, such as writing a report in a word processor, producing accounts in a spreadsheet program or editing a picture in a painting program.

A new smartphone, tablet, laptop, etc., usually contains some pre-installed applications or *apps*. Operating systems such as Windows, Android and iOS also provide many useful apps, such as a Web browser, basic word processor and drawing and painting programs.

Although many apps, i.e. programs, may be pre-installed on a new computer, you may want to install additional apps for your personal interests. This might include a specialist Desktop Publishing (DTP) program, a sophisticated drawing and painting program, or a game you wish to play.

Previously most software was bought on a magnetic disc or on a CD. Nowadays programs are usually bought online, *downloaded* from a Web server on the Internet, i.e. the Clouds and permanently saved on the Internal Storage of your smartphone, tablet, laptop or desktop.

Alternatively, most operating systems include an *app store* on the Internet from which you can *download* apps and save them permanently on your computer. Many of the apps in the apps stores are free. Well-known apps stores are the **Microsoft Store**, (Windows), the **Google Play Store** (Android) and the **App Store** (iOS — iPhone, iPad, etc.)

Windows 10

Android

iOS

The Web Browser

The Web browser is used to find and retrieve information from a Web site and display it on your computer. The browser is an app usually pre-installed on a new computer.

Web browsers provided with the main operating systems are:

- Microsoft Edge and Internet Explorer:(Windows)
- Google Chrome: (Android)
- Safari: (iOS and macOS)

If you don't like the browser installed by default on a new computer you can replace it with one of the others, which can generally be installed on all the main operating systems, i.e. Windows, Android and iOS and macOS. In addition, Mozilla Firefox and Opera are popular browsers which can be installed on the main operating systems.

Each Web site has a unique address such as:

www.babanibooks.com

After typing the address into the address bar on the browser, the Home or opening page of the Web site is displayed.

The Search Engine

If you don't know the address of a Web site, you can search for it by typing *keywords* into a program called a *search engine*. After entering one or more keywords, a list of Web sites containing the keywords is displayed. Each entry in the list is a *link* to open a Web site.

Well-known search engines include Google, Yahoo! and Bing. A default search engine is pre-installed on a new computer but you can change this if you wish.

Browsing and searching are discussed in detail in Chapters 3 and 4.

Your Own Website on the Internet

Using a Web Host

If you want to set up your own website, perhaps to share information or promote a small business, you can pay to rent space for your website on a server provided by a *Web hosting* company.

Creating a Website

Web pages are written in a special language called HTML (Hypertext Markup Language). You can buy software, i.e. programs, to design your own website. Or you can entrust the work to a skilled *Web page designer*.

The Website Address

As mentioned earlier, every website has a unique address to enable Web browsers to find it. You need to make up a *domain name* such as **myownwebsite.com** and then pay to register it with an organisation called a *domain name registrar*. Alternatively some Web hosts offer free domain name registration.

Since the Web address has to be a unique identifier, the registrar will check to see whether your chosen domain name has already been taken. The Web address is also known as a *URL (Uniform Resource Locator)*. The full address might be something like:

http://www.myownwebsite.com

Or: **https://www.myonlinestore.com**

https (rather than http) shown above denotes a *secure website*. This is discussed in more detail in Chapter 3.

3

Safe Websites

Introduction

As mentioned in Chapter 2, a Web browser is the software used to access websites and view Web pages. Well-known browsers are Google Chrome, Safari, Internet Explorer, Microsoft Edge, Firefox and Opera.

A new computer will normally have one of the above browsers preinstalled. For example, the Android operating system uses Google Chrome while Windows has Internet Explorer and Microsoft Edge. The Apple iOS operating system (iPhones and iPads) uses the Safari browser. Web browsers are *apps* with versions available for all of the main operating systems. So, for example, some Windows users may prefer to install the Firefox browser instead of Microsoft Edge, provided with Window 10.

Many of the activities carried out while you are browsing or "surfing the net" provide opportunities for hackers and fraudsters. Such activities include:

- Checking your bank account online and making payments and funds transfers.
- Buying goods and services online using a debit or credit card.
- Using social networks like Facebook and Twitter involving your private and personal information.
- Sending and receiving e-mails. (Some e-mail systems use a Web browser while others use a program called an *e-mail client*).

Connecting to a Website

Click or tap the icon for your particular Web browser, such as Google Chrome for example, as shown below.

| Google Chrome | Apple Safari | Microsoft Edge | Internet. Explorer | Mozilla Firefox | Opera |

Across the top of the browser is the *Address Bar* shown below.

Entering the Address of a Website

If you know the address of a website you wish to view, you can type it into the Address Bar as shown below.

On suitably equipped computers you might prefer to tap the microphone icon shown on the right and speak the address of the website.

Pressing **Enter** or **Return** or selecting the **Go** button shown on the right opens the *Home Page* of the website, as shown on the next page. Note the **Address Bar** for **ebay** across the top of the page and a **Search Bar** lower down. The **Address Bar** and **Search Bar** are very similar, but used in different ways, as discussed shortly.

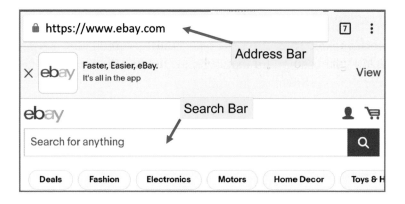

The address of a website as shown above and below is also known as a *URL* (*Uniform Resource Locator*).

🔒 **https://www.ebay.com**

Using the Keyword Search to Find a Website

Suppose you don't know the address or URL of a website, or you want to find information on a particular subject. You can usually find what you want by entering *keywords*, into the search bar in the browser. Keywords identify the subject matter you are interested in, such as **green woodpecker**, for example. Alternatively the keywords can be entered into the address bar of your browser, such as Google Chrome, Safari or Firefox.

Search engines like Google App, Microsoft Bing and Yahoo! can be used as part of a Web browser or as a separate, standalone app. Yahoo! is based on Bing.

For example, to find information about the **green woodpecker**, enter the keywords into the search bar or the address bar, as shown below. Then select the search icon shown on the right.

Alternatively you can speak the keywords after selecting the microphone icon. Google returns a very long list of millions of results as shown below.

19,600,000 search results

About 19,600,000 results (0.68 seconds)

Green Woodpecker Facts | Picus Viridis - The RSPB
https://www.rspb.org.uk/birds-and-wildlife/wildlife-guides/bird.../green-woodpecker ▾
The green woodpecker is the largest of the three woodpeckers that breed in Britain. It has a heavy-looking body, short tail and a strong, long bill. It is green on its ...

People also search for
uk woodpecker   great spotted woodpecker call
green woodpecker laughing call   green woodpecker in winter
another name for green woodpecker   grey headed woodpecker

European green woodpecker - Wikipedia
https://en.wikipedia.org/wiki/European_green_woodpecker ▾
The European green woodpecker (Picus viridis) is a member of the woodpecker family Picidae. The

Please Note: Google and Google Chrome

- Google or Google App is a *search engine* used for keyword searches as described above and on page 21.
- Google Chrome is a Web *browser* used for viewing and moving around Web pages.

The words in blue text below and on the previous page are *links* or *hyperlinks* which connect you to Web pages containing the keywords.

Green Woodpecker Facts | Picus Viridis - The RSPB
https://www.rspb.org.uk/birds-and-wildlife/wildlife-guides/bird.../green-
The **green woodpecker** is the largest of the three woodpeckers that breed

---

The Web pages at the top of the list are generally the most relevant to the search. Click or tap a link to open the corresponding website.

Tapping or clicking the blue text link at the top of the results list on the previous page and shown again above opens the Home Page of the RSPB website shown below.

The previous keyword search was carried out using the Google Chrome browser, on a Windows desktop computer. However, keyword searching is done in a similar way on other browsers and search engines such as Safari, Firefox, Microsoft Edge and Internet Explorer and on all types of computer from smartphones to desktop machines. Shown below is the result of the previous search but this time executed and displayed on an Android smartphone.

Please Note: Web Address or Keyword Search

- Entering an *address* into the *address bar* of a browser takes you straight to the Home Page of the website.

- Typing *keywords* into the *search bar* produces a long list of links to websites containing the keywords.

Data Privacy

When you first open the Home Page of a large organisation you will see a statement asking you to accept the use of *cookies*. Or a statement saying that by continuing on the website you have accepted the use of cookies. As discussed in more detail on the next page, cookies are small text files intended to personalise the service provided to you by the website. You may also be told that by not accepting cookies, you will not get the full website services.

Websites for large organisations should also have a link which can be used to display their *privacy policy*. This should outline the steps that the organisation takes to keep your data safe. The privacy policy should comply with *GDPR*, recent data protection legislation discussed below.

GDPR

This is the *General Data Protection Regulation*, a legal document enforced in Europe on 25th May 2018 and intended to protect the data privacy of individuals. Amongst other things, large organisations with websites must use clear, plain and intelligible language to:

- Obtain your *consent* to use your personal data.
- Provide you with copies of your personal data and correct any mistakes if it's not accurate.
- Delete your personal data if requested by you.
- Change the way your data is used if you ask them to.
- Obtain your consent to send, or continue sending you, e-mails containing advertising, etc.
- Inform you if your data privacy has been breached.

Cookies

- A *cooki*e is a small text file, which stores information about you and your browsing activities.

- Cookies are stored on the *client,* i.e. your computer, by the server and are accessible to the *server*, i.e. the computer hosting the website you are visiting.

- Cookies save time because you don't need to re-enter your personal details every time you visit the website.

- A cookie allows the server to tailor what is displayed based on your previous visits to the website.

- Some websites require you to agree to cookies being used before you continue on the site. Or you are informed that by continuing it is assumed that you are happy for cookies to be used.

- *Session* cookies are deleted when you close a website. *Persistent* cookies remain for a specified time or until you delete them from your hard disk or Internal Storage.

- A *third-party cookie* is stored on your computer by a website other than the one you are visiting. Browsers such as Chrome and Firefox allow you to block third-party cookies.

- Some people find cookies an invasion of their privacy, especially *tracking cookies*, which may be used to collect your browsing details and interests which can then be used for advertising.

- If you switch off standard, i.e. first-party, cookies in the **Settings** in your browser, you may find some websites can no longer be fully used.

- Deleting cookies and other files saved on your computer as part of your *browsing history* is discussed in Chapter 5.

Security: The Padlock Icon

🔒 https://www.ebay.com

http

Some Web sites use *http* rather than *https* shown above. http stands for *hypertext transfer protocol*. Hypertext is text which allows links to other pieces of text or webpages. Transfer protocol refers to a set of rules which control the exchange of data between different devices.

When you request information such as Web pages from a Web server, it is sent across the Internet in small *packets* before being re-assembled and viewed on your computer.

With http, the data is transferred as plain text. So a hacker getting access to your computer would be able to see whatever data you are sending or receiving and use it for criminal purposes such as identity theft.

https

The **s** in **https** above refers to a *secure website,* used for sending and receiving important personal data in activities such as online banking and shopping. The data between your computer and a secure website is *encrypted* or *scrambled*. This means the data can only be unscrambled and read using a secret string of numbers known as a *private key*. Encryption and decryption are controlled by the Web server, which also stores the private key.

Without the private key, a hacker gaining access to the network between your computer and a secure server will not be able to read the data.

Shown below is the address bar in Google Chrome on a Windows desktop computer.

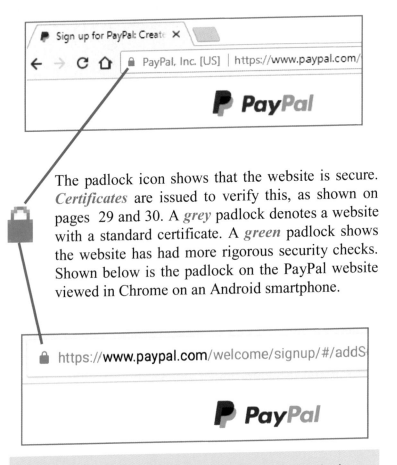

The padlock icon shows that the website is secure. *Certificates* are issued to verify this, as shown on pages 29 and 30. A *grey* padlock denotes a website with a standard certificate. A *green* padlock shows the website has had more rigorous security checks. Shown below is the padlock on the PayPal website viewed in Chrome on an Android smartphone.

Always check that a website has a padlock icon, preferably green, as shown in the address bars above, before signing up for an account and entering your personal data such as name, address and bank account details.

If you view a website that is not secure, the browser should display a warning, instead of the grey or green padlock.

Shown below are the three possible icons for a website viewed in Google Chrome, currently the most popular Web browser. Depending on the security rating of the website, one of these icons will appear to the left of the address, as shown on the previous page, in the Chrome browser.

Tap or click whichever icon appears on the address bar. This displays more information about the security of the website, as shown below in Google Chrome.

The **Certificate** listed on the previous page and shown below opened in Google Chrome has been verified as secure by a *trusted certification authority*.

The certification authorities are worldwide hitech organisations — companies such as Verizon, now part of Symantec, one of the world's leading cyber security software companies and discussed in Chapter 11.

Clicking or tappng the padlock icon is also the standard method to view the security information of a website on other browsers such as Safari, Firefox, Edge, Internet Explorer, etc., as well as Google Chrome just discussed.

Browsing Basics

Introduction

Chapter 3 discussed the various Web browsers and also:

- Connecting to a website by entering the address or by selecting it from a list after a keyword search.

- Checking the level of security of a site after selecting the padlock icon, shown on the right.

- Also website cookies and the implications of the GDPR legislation for the ordinary computer user.

This chapter discusses browsing or surfing around the Internet. Popular browsers such as Chrome, Safari, Firefox and Internet Explorer all use similar icons for the main browsing tasks on smartphones, tablets and larger computers. The Safari examples were carried out on iPads and iPhones but Safari on the MacBook is very similar.

The remainder of this chapter describes the management of Favourites and Bookmarks (essentially the same), used to save time when revisiting websites.

Chapter 5 covers Web information which is saved automatically on your computer, such as your Browsing History, the Cache of saved Web pages and Cookies. Cookies are saved by websites wishing to know your preferences and possibly target you with advertising.

To protect your privacy and to save storage space, your History, Cache, Cookies, Favourites and Bookmarks should be deleted when no longer needed, as discussed in Chapter 5.

Moving Between Pages

Links or Hyperlinks

After you arrive at the Home Page of a website, as discussed in Chapter 3, you may wish to move to other Web pages to view more information.

On a Windows computer, as you move the cursor around the screen, you'll notice that the cursor changes from an arrow to a hand when it's over certain screen objects, such as pieces of text or pictures. The appearance of the hand indicates a *link*, also known as a *hyperlink*. While the cursor is over a text link the words are underlined as shown below.

> hy Hedgehog Street was born. It's all
> ve *our favourite wild animal* (N.B. The
> h deciding this)

On touchscreen devices, text links are normally in a different colour from the rest of the text, as shown by the blue links below.

Click or tap a link to move to another Web page, which may be in another part of the current Web site. Or it may be on a different Web site on another Web server anywhere in the world.

Browser Buttons

Browsers such as Chrome, Safari, Internet Explorer and Edge use buttons and icons the same or similar to those shown below on Firefox, to help with browsing.

Firefox

 The arrows allow you to move forward and back between the Web pages you've visited.

 The *Refresh* button shown on the left displays the latest version of a Web page.

 This icon takes you back to the Home or starting page of the website.

The padlock icon shown on the left and above is very important in verifying the security of a website and discussed in detail in Chapter 3.

Similar icons appear near the top of the Safari screen, as shown below.

Safari

You may need to tap the Menu button shown on the right, to display the Home icon shown above.

Revisiting Web Pages

Favourites and Bookmarks

To revisit a Web page in the future with a single tap or click, you can save it in a list as a *Bookmark* or a *Favourite*. These are essentially the same.

Chrome and Firefox use Bookmarks while Internet Explorer and Edge use Favourites (spelt as Favorite in American English). Safari uses both Favourites and Bookmarks.

Your Reading List

As shown on page 38, Safari provides a *Reading List* icon when you want to save a Web page to read later, perhaps offline. Once you've read the page it is deleted from your Reading List.

Your Browser History

This is a list of Web pages that you've visited. The History list is recorded automatically. This saves you typing the Web address in again if you want to revisit the site. A website you've entered may have needed a password and other personal information and this is also saved.

The Web Cache

When a Web page is opened in your browser for the first time, a copy of the page is saved in an area of your hard disk known as the *cache*. Next time you access the Web page it opens much faster. The page recovered from the cache may not always be the latest version. Click or tap the **Refresh** button shown on the right to display the latest version of a Web page, including any updates since your last visit.

Android Smartphones and Tablets

Saving Bookmarks

Chrome and Firefox Browsers

The Chrome and Firefox browsers look very similar on Android smartphones and tablets as shown below.

- Tap the 3-dot menu button, shown on the right and below, on the top right of the Web page.

- Tap the Bookmark star icon which appears, as shown on the left below.

```
🔒 https://www.rspb.org.uk/birds    9    ⋮
```

Firefox Browser	Chrome Browser
← → ☆ ⟳	→ ☆ ⬇ ⓘ ⟳
Share >	New tab
New Tab	New incognito tab **Security Of Website**
New Private Tab	Bookmarks
Bookmarks	Recent tabs
History	History

- After tapping to save the Bookmark, the icon is filled with blue.

Android Smartphones and Tablets

Viewing Bookmarks

Chrome and Firefox Browsers

- In Chrome or Firefox select the 3-dot menu at the top right of the screen.

- Then tap **Bookmarks** from the menu which appears, as shown below.

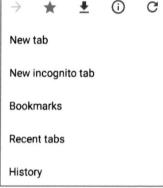

Firefox Browser   Chrome Browser

- The list of **Bookmarks** is displayed, as shown in the small samples below.

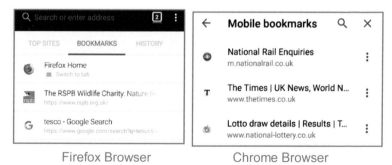

Firefox Browser   Chrome Browser

Android Smartphones and Tablets

Deleting Bookmarks

Chrome Browser

- Tap the 3-dot menu button at the top right of the screen.
- Tap **Bookmarks** as shown on the previous page.
- Tap the 3-dot menu button at the right of the Bookmark to be deleted, as shown below.
- Select **Delete** from the pop-up menu as shown below.

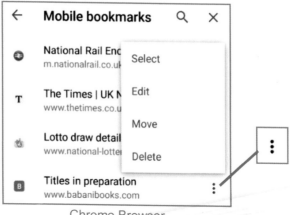

Chrome Browser

Firefox Browser

- Tap the 3-dot menu button at the top right of the screen.
- Tap **Bookmarks**.
- *Tap and hold* the Bookmark to be deleted.
- Select **Remove** from the menu which pops up.

iPhones and iPads
Saving Bookmarks and Favourites
Safari Browser

- Tap the icon shown on the right and below then select either **Add Bookmark** or **Add to Favourites**.

- Select **Add Bookmark** as shown above, then **Save** as shown on the left below, to add a link to a website to the **Bookmarks** list, shown on the next page.

- Alternatively, as shown below, the link can be added to the **Favourites** folder or the **Favourites Bar**.

iPhones and iPads

Viewing Bookmarks and Favourites

Safari Browser

- Tap the book icon shown on the right and on the screenshot below.

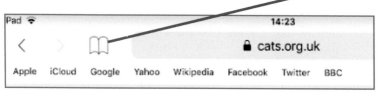

- The **Bookmarks** panel opens on the left of the screen, as shown below. Or select the + icon shown on page 38 to view icons of your Favourites, as shown on the right below.

- Tap on a Bookmark in the list to revisit the Web page, or select the icon in the Favourites screen shown on the right above.

iPhones and iPads
Deleting Bookmarks and Favourites

Safari Browser

- Open the **Bookmarks/Favourites** panel after tapping the icon shown on the right. To display all of your Bookmarks and Favourites as shown below, tap **Favourites** shown at the bottom of the previous page.

‹ Bookmarks **Favourites**
📖   OO   ⊙
📖 Apple
📖 iCloud
📖 Google
📖 The RSPB Wildlife Charity: Nat...
📖 3 Ways to Cool Your Cat Down...
📖 Cats Protection - UK's Largest...
📖 Watch ITV live - ITV Hub
Edit

- Tap **Edit** at the bottom of the screen to display the red minus icon shown below, at the side of each item.

- Tap the red minus sign icon.
- Tap the **Delete** button which appears. This removes the Bookmark or Favourite .
- Tap **Done** to finish.

Windows PCs
Saving Bookmarks and Favourites
Chrome, Firefox, Internet Explorer, Edge Browsers

As mentioned earlier, Favourites and Bookmarks are basically the same. The general method in all of the above browsers is:

- Tap the star icon, at the top right of the browser screen, shown below.

- Enter a name for the Bookmark or Favourite, choose a folder to save it in then select **Done**.

Saving a Bookmark on Chrome Browser

Saving a Favourite on Internet Explorer Browser

Windows PC
Viewing and Deleting Bookmarks
Chrome Browser

- Click the 3-dot menu button shown below.
- Select **Bookmarks**.

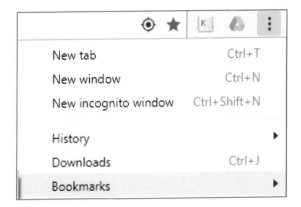

- Select **Mobile bookmarks** to see all of your bookmarks from all of your devices.

- Click a Bookmark to revisit the Web page.

- Right-click and select **Delete** to remove the Bookmark.

Windows PC
Viewing and Deleting Bookmarks

Firefox Browser

- Click the **Library** icon shown on the right.   ꘓ

- Select **Bookmarks** shown below.

- If necessary, select **Show All Bookmarks** shown below.

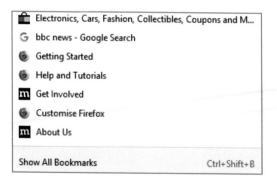

- Click a Bookmark to revisit the Web page.

- Right-click and select **Delete** to remove the Bookmark.

Windows PC

Viewing and Deleting Favourites

Internet Explorer Browser

- Click the icon shown on the right and below.
- Select **Favourites** shown below.

- Click a Favourite to revisit the Web page.
- Right-click and select **Delete** to remove the Favourite.

Microsoft Edge Browser

- Click the **Hub** icon shown on the right.
- Select **Favourites** in the left-hand panel in the window which opens.
- Click a Favourite to revisit the Web page.
- Right-click and select **Delete** to remove the Favourite.

Clearing Browsing Data

Introduction

Bookmarks and Favourites discussed in the last chapter are saved deliberately by the user, unlike *browsing data*, discussed in this chapter, which is saved automatically by the computer. Browsing data consists of:

- Your *History* or the list of websites you've visited.
- *Cookies* or files recording your bowsing habits.
- The *Web Cache*, i.e. Web pages stored on your hard disc, to speed up revisiting a website in the

Browsing data may be useful to a parent or grandparent wanting to make sure a child is not visiting undesirable websites. The police make extensive use of browsing records and e-mails, etc., in solving crimes.

Conversely, your browsing data might make you a target for unwelcome advertising or attract fraudsters looking to steal your savings. Or you might wish to keep private the fact that you've been researching online a serious health problem or arranging a surprise holiday or present.

Clearing Your Browsing Data

As well as privacy and security issues just discussed, saving browsing data such as the cache takes up valuable storage on your computer and may cause it to run slowly.

So it's a good idea to clear obsolete browsing data, as discussed in the rest of this chapter.

Android Smartphones and Tablets
Clearing Browsing Data
Chrome Browser

- Tap the 3-dot menu button at the top right of the screen. ⋮

- Select **History** from the menu which appears as shown below.

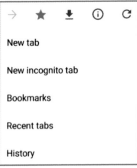

- This opens the **History** window shown below.

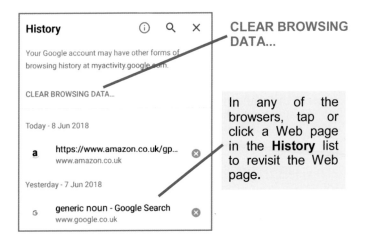

CLEAR BROWSING DATA...

In any of the browsers, tap or click a Web page in the **History** list to revisit the Web page.

Android Smartphones and Tablets

Clearing Browsing Data

Chrome Browser

(Continued from page 46)

- Tap **CLEAR BROWSING DATA...** shown on the previous page. This opens the window shown below.

← **Clear browsing data**   ❓

BASIC   ADVANCED

Time range   All time   ▾

🕐   **Browsing history**
       7 items (and more on synced
       devices)   ☑

🍪   **Cookies and site data**
       From 240 sites   ☑

🖼   **Cached images and files**
       68.0 MB   ☑

                                    CLEAR DATA

- Tap the arrow next to **All time** shown above, then choose the **Time range** over which the data is to be deleted.

- Tick the boxes shown in blue above to select the data to be deleted.

- Tap **CLEAR DATA** at the bottom right of the window shown above.

Last hour

Last 24 Hours

Last 7 days

Last 4 weeks

All time

Android Smartphones and Tablets

Clearing Browsing Data

Firefox Browser

- The Firefox **HISTORY** panel shown below is opened in the same way as described on page 46 for the Chrome browser.

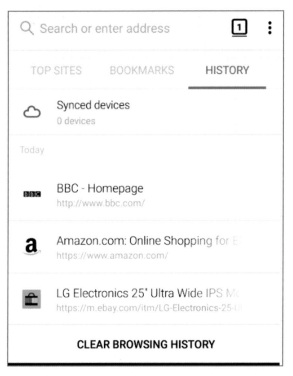

- Select **CLEAR BROWSING HISTORY** shown above to remove the list of websites you've visited.

Android Smartphones and Tablets

Clearing Browsing Data

Firefox Browser
(Continued from page 48)

- Select the 3-dot menu button at the top right of ⋮ the screen.
- Scroll down the menu and select **Settings**.
- From the **Settings** menu, select **Clear private data** to open the menu shown below.

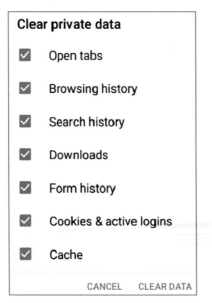

Clear private data

- ☑ Open tabs
- ☑ Browsing history
- ☑ Search history
- ☑ Downloads
- ☑ Form history
- ☑ Cookies & active logins
- ☑ Cache

CANCEL   CLEAR DATA

- Tick the items you wish to clear, such as your **Browsing history**, your **Search history**, **Cookies** and the **Cache** of saved Web pages, as shown above
- Tap CLEAR DATA shown above on the bottom right.

iPhones and iPads

Clearing Browsing Data

Safari Browser

- To clear the **History**, i.e, the list of websites visited and other browsing data, open Safari and tap the book icon shown on the right.

- If necessary, tap the clock icon shown on the right and below to open the **History** list shown above.

- Tap Clear at the bottom right of the **History** list shown above to open the menu shown on the next page.

iPhones and iPads

Clearing Browsing Data

Safari Browser
(continued from page 50)

- Select the time period shown below, over which to remove **History**, cookies and other browsing data.

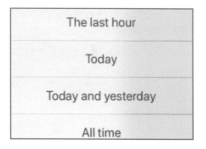

| The last hour |
| Today |
| Today and yesterday |
| All time |

- Alternatively tap the **Settings** icon shown on the right, located on the Home Screen.

- Tap **Safari** on the left-hand side of the **Settings** screen then tap Clear History and Website Data in the right-hand panel.

- Then tap Clear from the small window which appears, as shown below, to remove *all* of your **history, cookies and other browsing data**.

Clear History and Data

Clearing will remove history, cookies and other browsing data.

History will be cleared from devices signed in to your iCloud account.

| Cancel | Clear |

Windows PC

Clearing Browsing Data

Chrome Browser

- Select the 3-dot menu button at the top right of the screen. ⋮
- Select **More tools** from the drop-down menu which appears and then select **Clear browsing data...**.
- This opens the **Clear browsing data** window, as shown below.

Clear browsing data   ✕

Basic   Advanced

Time range   Last hour   ▾

☑   Browsing history
    Clears history and autocompletions in the address bar. Your Google account
    may have other forms of browsing history at myactivity.google.com.

☑   Cookies and other site data
    Signs you out of most sites.

☑   Cached images and files
    Frees up less than 331 MB. Some sites may load more slowly on your next
    visit.

                                    CANCEL   **CLEAR DATA**

- Make sure the data you wish to remove is marked with ticks, as shown above.

Windows PC

Clearing Browsing Data

Chrome Browser
(Continued from page 52)

- Tap the small arrow to the right of **Time range**, shown above, to choose a time period .

- Finally select **CLEAR DATA** as shown at the bottom of page 52.

Firefox Browser

- Tap the **Library** icon shown on the right and select **History**, shown below.

Windows PC

Clearing Browsing Data

Firefox Browser
(Continued from page 53)

- The **History** window pops up showing the **Recent History** of Web pages visited, with an option to **Show All History**. Tap a Web page in the list if you want to revisit it.

- Tap **Clear Recent History...** at the top of the **History** window, as shown below.

- From the **Clear Recent History** window shown below, set the **Time range to clear**.

- Tick the boxes against the **History** data to be cleared, such as **Cookies** and **Cache** shown below.

- Select **Clear Now** shown below to remove the data.

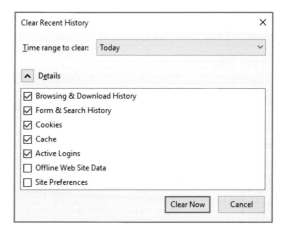

Windows PC

Clearing Browsing Data

Internet Explorer Browser

- Select **Tools** (the gear icon) at the top right of the screen.

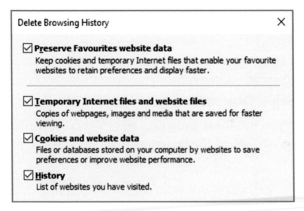

- Select **Safety** then **Delete browsing history...** to open the window shown in part below.

- Tick the boxes next to the data you wish to remove. (**Temporary Internet files...** above refers to the *Cache* discussed on page 34.)

- Finally select **Delete** shown below. This appears at the bottom of the **Delete Browsing History** window partly shown above.

Windows PC

Clearing Browsing Data

Microsoft Edge Browser

- Tap the **Hub** icon shown on the right. ☆≡
- Select **History** on the left below.

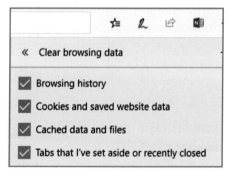

- Select **Clear history** shown on the right above.
- From the **Clear browsing data** window, shown in part below, select the browsing data you wish to remove.

- Finally select **Clear** at the bottom of the **Clear browsing data** window to remove the data.

Private Browsing

Introduction

Chapter 5 discussed the way to clear our *browsing data*, the trail of information we leave behind during a browsing session. However, unless you clear your browsing data straightaway, other people with access to your computer, can still see what you've been doing.

Private browsing enables you to browse the Web without leaving a trail of data about yourself and your browsing habits. All of the main browsers such as Chrome, Safari, Firefox, Internet Explorer, Microsoft Edge, etc., allow private browsing, although it may be known under another name, such as *Privacy Mode* or *Incognito Mode*. Private browsing works in a similar way in most browsers.

Data which is *not saved* after private browsing includes:

- The History list of Web pages visited.
- Criteria entered in a Search bar.
- Data entered in on-screen forms and passwords.
- Certain types of cookies used to track your visits across websites.
- Cached Web pages and Temporary Internet Files.

Data which remains after private browsing includes:

- Bookmarks or Favourites which you create.
- Files downloaded to your computer from the Web.

In private browsing, the borders around a Web page are often black or darker than in normal browsing mode.

Android Smartphones and Tablets

Incognito Browsing (i.e. Private Browsing)

Chrome Browser

- Tap the 3-dot menu button at the top right of the Chrome browser screen.

- Select **New incognito tab** from the menu which appears as shown below.

- This opens the New **incognito tab** shown below.

The screenshot above was taken on an Android tablet. A similar incognito screen appears on an Android phone. The methods described for tablets on the next page are broadly similar to those used on Android phones.

Android Smartphones and Tablets

Incognito Browsing

Chrome Browser

(Continued from page 58)

The **New incognito tab** on the previous page informs you that your browsing history, search history and cookies won't be around after you close your incognito tabs. Your file downloads and the bookmarks you create will be kept.

Using Incognito Browsing

- Enter the search keyword(s) or Web address (URL) in the Address bar shown below on an Android tablet.

- Then continue browsing as described in Chapter 4.

- Tap the hat and spectacles icon shown on the right, to switch incognito mode On or Off.

Closing Incognito Browsing

Android Tablet

- Tap the **X** in the tab at the top left above and also shown below to close a tab.

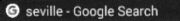

Android Phone

- Tap the *tab button* shown on the right, to display all open tabs.

- Then tap the 3-dot menu button and select **Close incognito tabs**.

Android Smartphones and Tablets

Private Browsing

Firefox Browser

- Tap the 3-dot menu button at the top right of the Firefox browser screen. ⫶
- Select **New Private Tab** from the menu which appears.
- The **Private Browsing** screen opens as shown below.

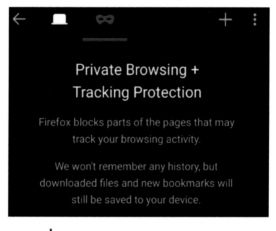

- Tap the **+** icon to open a new tab or window.
- The search bar at the top of the screen is now black.

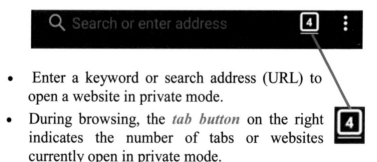

- Enter a keyword or search address (URL) to open a website in private mode.
- During browsing, the *tab button* on the right indicates the number of tabs or websites currently open in private mode.

Android Smartphones and Tablets

Private Browsing

Firefox Browser

(Continued from page 60)

- To view thumbnails of the currently open private tabs, tap the numeric tab button shown on the right and on page 60. This opens the screen shown in part below.

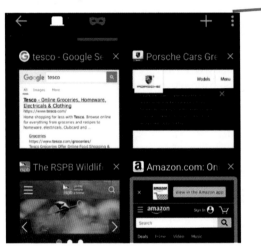

- Tap on a thumbnail to open it full screen.
- Tap **X** at the top right of a tab to close it.
- Use the icons shown on the right to switch between thumbnails of websites currently open in either private or normal browsing.
- Tap the 3-dot menu button shown on the right and above and then select **Close Private Tabs** to return to non-private browsing.

iPhones and iPads

Private Browsing

Safari Browser

The methods used for private browsing are the same on the iPhone and iPad. Both use the same icons and buttons, but they are located in different parts of the screen. The layouts below are based on the iPhone.

Turning Private Browsing On
- Tap the compass icon shown above to open Safari.
- Tap the **Tabs** button at the bottom right of the screen, shown on the right and below. On the iPad this appears at the top right of the screen.

- Tap **Private** at the bottom left of the screen, as shown below. On the iPad this appears at the top right.

- After selecting **Private**, the **Private Browsing Mode** notice appears, as shown below.

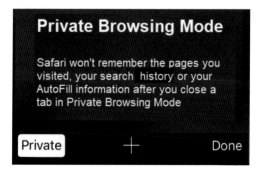

iPhones and iPads

Private Browsing
Safari Browser
(Continued from page 62)

- Tap **Done,** shown at the bottom of page 62, then start private browsing by entering some keywords or a website address in the search bar, as shown below.

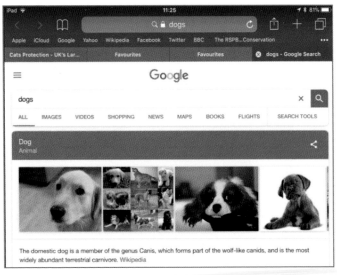

- As shown above, Web page headers are black in **Private Browsing Mode** instead of the usual grey in normal mode, as shown in the middle of page 62.

Turning Off Private Browsing

- To turn off private browsing, tap the **Tabs** button shown on the right, then tap **Private** and **Done,** shown below.

Windows PC

Incognito Browsing (i.e. Private Browsing)

Chrome Browser

- Click the icon shown above to open Chrome, then click the 3-dot menu button at the top right of the screen and select **New incognito window**.

- Alternatively, from Chrome, press **Ctrl+Shift+n**.

- The black Incognito window opens with the notice shown below, explaining Incognito browsing.

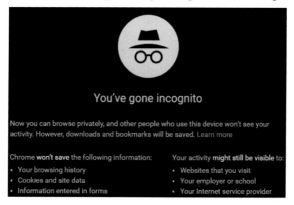

- To start Incognito browsing enter a Web address (URL) or keyword(s) in the search bar at the top of the screen, as shown below.

- To close Incognito browsing click the **X** on the tab as shown above.

Windows PC

Private Browsing
Firefox Browser

- Click the icon shown above to open Firefox, then click the 3-bar menu button at the top right of the screen and select **New Private Window**.

- The **Private Browsing with Tracking Protection** window opens as shown below. Switching On Tracking Protection blocks parts of a Web page that might be used to monitor your browsing activities.

- To start Private Browsing enter a Web address (URL) or keyword(s) in the search bar at the top of the screen, as shown below.

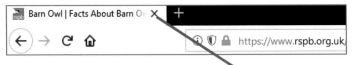

- To close Private Browsing click the **X** on the tab as shown above.

Windows PC
InPrivate Browsing
Internet Explorer Browser   Microsoft Edge Browser

The overall process of private browsing, known as **InPrivate Browsing** on the above two browsers, is very similar to the Chrome and Firefox browsers just described.

Opening InPrivate Browsing
Internet Explorer

- Click the gear icon at the top right of the Internet Explorer screen, then select **Safety** and **InPrivate Browsing**.

Microsoft Edge

- Click the menu button shown on the right at the top right of the screen and select **New InPrivate window**.

- Or to turn InPrivate browsing On in Internet Explorer or Microsoft Edge, press **Ctrl+Shift+p**.

- **InPrivate** now appears in the address bar, as shown on the right and below.

Turning InPrivate Browsing Off
To turn InPrivate browsing Off in both Internet Explorer and Microsoft Edge, click the cross **X** on the tab shown below.

Further Privacy Settings

Introduction

Chapter 5 discussed our *browsing data*, the trail of information we automatically leave behind during a browsing session. Unless you clear your browsing data straightaway, other people with access to your computer can see what you've been doing. So Chapter 5 explained how to clear all your browsing data.

Chapter 6 discussed *Private browsing*, available on all the main browsers such as Google Chrome, Apple Safari, Mozilla Firefox, Internet Explorer, Microsoft Edge, etc. Private browsing enables you to browse the Web without leaving a trail of data about yourself and your browsing habits. Data such as the History or list of sites visited, cookies, your searches and the cache of Web pages and temporary Internet files are cleared when you close the Web page or when you close the browser.

This chapter looks at some separate, individual settings in all of the browsers, intended to make your browsing more secure and private. These settings include:

- Blocking *cookies*, especially *third party cookies*.
- Requesting people or organisations not to *track you* across websites.
- Blocking *pop-ups* or adverts which suddenly appear, interrupting whatever you are doing.
- Stopping requests for your *location*, which may be quite legal but alternatively might be malicious.
- Warning you about or blocking *unsafe websites*.

Cookies

As mentioned elsewhere in this book, cookies are small text files containing your personal details and browsing habits, saved by websites on your Internal Storage or hard drive.

First Party Cookies

These are the standard cookies placed on your computer by the website you are visiting. They are intended to make your browsing experience better by remembering your personal details so that you don't have to keep entering data such as your e-mail address and password on every visit. Websites can also tailor the information they provide to you according to your previous browsing on the site.

When you first visit a website you are asked to accept the use of cookies or you are told that by proceeding you are, in fact, giving your agreement. Many websites won't function properly without the use of standard or first party cookies.

Third Party Cookies

These are cookies saved on your device by websites other than the one you have chosen to visit. Websites may welcome third party cookies from other websites because it generates extra income. Third party cookies are unpopular with some people because they may be used to target you for advertising rather than to improve your browsing experience on future visits.

Blocking Cookies

As discussed shortly, Web browsers have settings allowing you to either block or allow first and third party cookies. It is generally recommended that first party cookies should be allowed but some people now choose to block third party cookies, much to the disappointment of some advertising companies.

Tracking

Some websites may use cookies to analyse your browsing across multiple websites and then share your information with other companies who may target you with advertisements. All of the popular browsers have a *Do Not Track* option or similar, discussed shortly, which asks companies not to track you.

This is voluntary, so some websites may continue to track you. Some browsers, such as Firefox, have a built-in *Tracking Protection* feature which allows you to block websites that are known to track visitors.

Location Sharing

Some websites need your location to display the local map or tell someone where you are. Or if travelling with a mobile device such as a smartphone or tablet, your current **Location** may be used to find nearby facilities such as buses, hotels or petrol stations. **Location** is a **Privacy** option which can be turned off.

Blocking Pop-ups

Pop-ups are small windows which suddenly appear on the screen, causing annoyance when you're trying to do something else. Pop-ups may be advertisements (*adware*) or in some cases may have a criminal intent (*malware*). Most browsers include a pop-up blocker.

Accessing the settings for the above topics and cookies discussed on page 68 is described in the rest of this chapter for most of the popular browsers and computer platforms.

Android Smartphones and Tablets
Further Privacy Settings
Chrome Browser

- Tap the 3-dot menu button at the top right of the Chrome browser screen and select **Settings** followed by **Site settings**.

Cookies

- From the **Site settings** menu shown above, tap **Cookies**, then tap the buttons shown below, as required, to allow or disallow cookies and third-party cookies.

Android Smartphones and Tablets

Further Privacy Settings

Chrome Browser
(Continued from page 70)

Location

- Tap **Location** shown on page 70 and tap the button to switch **Ask before...** On or Off as required.

← Location	Q ⋮
Location
Ask before accessing (recommended)	

Pop-ups

- Tap **Pop-ups**, shown on page 70, to allow or block adverts, etc., which pop-up in windows on the screen.

← Pop-ups	Q ⋮
Pop-ups
Blocked (recommended)	

Do Not Track

- Tap the 3-dot menu button on the right and select **Settings** and **Privacy** tap to switch "**Do Not Track**" On or Off as required.

Safe Browsing

- From the **Settings>Privacy** menu make sure **Safe Browsing** is ticked, as shown below.

| Safe Browsing
Protect you and your device from dangerous sites	☑

Android Smartphones and Tablets

Further Privacy Settings

Firefox Browser

- Tap the 3-dot menu button at the top right of the Firefox browser screen.

- Tap **Settings** and then **Privacy** to open the menu shown in part below.

← **Privacy**

Do not track
Firefox will tell sites that you do not want to be tracked

Learn more ›

Tracking Protection
Enabled in Private Browsing

Learn more ›

Cookies
Enabled

Android Smartphones and Tablets

Further Privacy Settings

Firefox Browser

(Continued from page 72)

Do Not Track

- Tap the button shown on the **Privacy** menu on the previous page to switch the **Do not track** request On or Off.

Tracking Protection

- Tap **Tracking Protection** shown on page 72 to open the sub-menu shown below. **Enabled in Private Browsing** is the default setting. Please also see the Firefox note at the bottom of this page.

Tracking Protection

○   Enabled

◉   Enabled in Private
      Browsing

○   Disabled   CANCEL

Private Browsing +
Tracking Protection

Firefox blocks parts of the pages that may
track your browsing activity.

Android Smartphones and Tablets
Further Privacy Settings

Firefox Browser
(Continued from page 73)
Cookies

- Tap **Cookies** shown on page 72 to open the sub-menu shown below. **Enabled** is the default setting.

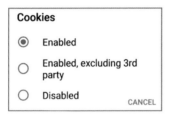

Location

- Scroll down the **Privacy** menu shown on page 72. Tick the box as shown in blue below to allow **Mozilla Location Service** to use your device's location as discussed on page 69.

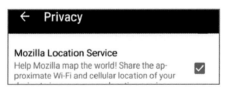

Pop-ups

Firefox for Android does not have a menu option to block pop-ups. However, Mozilla Firefox Support offer the following method for blocking pop-ups:

- Type **about:config** in the address bar.
- Enter **dom.disable_open_during_load** in Search.
- Set it to **false**. To re-enable pop-ups set to **true**.

iPhones and iPads
Further Privacy Settings
Safari Browser

- Tap the **Settings** icon shown on the right.
- The **Settings** menu opens. Tap **Safari** on the left-hand side of the screen.

Cookies

Shown below is part of the **PRIVACY & SECURITY** section of the Safari **Settings** menu.

Block Pop-ups	
PRIVACY & SECURITY	
Prevent Cross-Site Tracking	
Block All Cookies	
Ask Websites Not to Track Me	
Fraudulent Website Warning	

Depending on your version of the Apple iOS operating system, you will either see **Block All Cookies** shown above and below, or you will see **Block Cookies** Allow from Websit... >, the lower option shown below.

Block All Cookies

Block Cookies Allow from Websit... >

iPhones and iPads

Further Privacy Settings

Safari Browser

Cookies

(Continued from page 75)

- If your **Settings** menu displays **Block All Cookies** shown at the bottom of page 75, switching this On opens the notice shown below, advising caution.

- If your **Settings** menu displays **Block Cookies** Allow from Websit... > shown on page 75, tapping the button gives you a choice of which cookies to block or allow, as shown below.

Block Cookies	
COOKIES AND WEBSITE DATA	
Always Block	
Allow from Current Website Only	
Allow from Websites I Visit	✓
Always Allow	

iPhones and iPads
Further Privacy Settings
Safari Browser
Cookies
(Continued from page 76)

The default option **Allow from Websites I Visit**, shown ticked at the bottom of page 76, allows first party cookies and blocks third party cookies, as discussed on page 68. This is the setting favoured by a lot of users.

Pop-ups

- Tap the **Block Pop-ups** button on the Safari **Settings** menu shown again below to either allow or block adverts, etc., which pop-up on the screen.

Block Pop-ups	
PRIVACY & SECURITY	
Prevent Cross-Site Tracking	
Block All Cookies	
Ask Websites Not to Track Me	
Fraudulent Website Warning	

Tracking

- Switch On **Ask Websites Not to Track Me** shown above to send a request by Safari to a website you are visiting. The website may or may not honour your request.

iPhones and iPads

Further Privacy Settings

Safari Browser

Tracking
(Continued from page 77)

- The **Prevent Cross-Site Tracking** button shown on page 77 should be switched On, if you want to stop third-party content providers tracking you across websites to advertise products and services.

Fraudulent Website

- Tap the **Fraudulent Website Warning** button, shown on page 77, if you want Safari to display a warning if a site is suspected of *phishing*.

Phishing is the stealing of information such as your bank account details and usernames and passwords. Safari can check websites with Safe Browsing organisations.

Location Services

This uses GPS, Wi-Fi and cell phone networks to determine the location of you and your device. This can then be used to find nearby cafes, hotels, businesses, etc.

- Tap the **Settings** icon then select **Privacy** and tap the green button shown below to switch **Location Services** On or Off.

‹ Privacy	**Location Services**

Location Services

Location Services uses Bluetooth and crowd-sourced Wi-Fi hotspot locations to determine your approximate location.
About Location Services & Privacy

Windows PC

Further Privacy Settings

Chrome Browser

- Click the icon shown above to open Chrome, then click the 3-dot menu button at the top right of the screen and select **Settings** from the menu.

- Select **Settings** again but now from the 3-line button at the top left of the screen.   ≡ Settings

- Click **Advanced** then **Privacy and Security**.

Tracking

- From the **Privacy and security** menu switch "Do Not Track" On or Off as required, as shown below.

Privacy and security

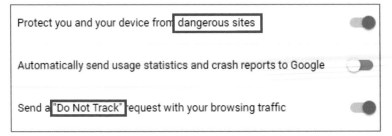

Dangerous Websites

- Click the top right button shown above to switch protection from **dangerous sites** On or Off as required.

Windows PC

Further Privacy Settings

Chrome Browser

(Continued from page 79)

Cookies

- From the **Privacy and security** menu shown in part on page 79, scroll down and select **Content Settings...**.

- Tap **Cookies** to see the options for switching **Cookies** On or Off, as shown below.

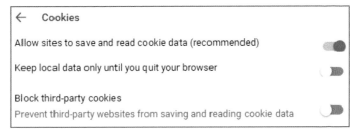

Location

- From the **Content Settings...** menu, below **Cookies**, click **Location**. Use the button to switch **Ask before accessing (recommended)** On or Off.

Pop-ups

- From the **Content Settings ...** menu, scroll down and use the button to block pop-ups (recommended).

Windows PC

Further Privacy Settings

Firefox Browser

- Click the icon shown above to open Firefox and then select the menu button shown on the right. Next click **Options** and **Privacy & Security**. This opens the **Privacy & Security** menu shown in part below.

Cookies and Site Data

Your stored cookies, site data and cache are currently using 53.6 MB of disc space. Learn more

- Accept cookies and site data from web sites (recommended)

  Keep until | They expire | ▼ |

  Accept third-party cookies and site data | Always | ▼ |

- Block cookies and site data (may cause web sites to break)

Cookies

- The **Cookies and Site Data** section of the **Privacy & Security** menu shown above allows you to accept (recommended) or block cookies from websites.

- You can choose whether to accept or block third party cookies.

- You can also select whether to keep cookies until they expire or until you close the Firefox browser.

Windows PC

Further Privacy Settings

Firefox Browser
(Continued from page 81)

Tracking

- From the **Privacy &Security** menu discussed on page 81, scroll down to the **Tracking Protection** section.

Tracking Protection

Tracking Protection blocks online trackers that collect your browsing data across multiple web sites.

Learn more about Tracking Protection and your privacy

Use Tracking Protection to block known trackers

   Always

 ⦿ Only in private windows

Exceptions...

Change Block List...

- The menu shown above has options to block known trackers from following you across multiple sites.
- Also to send websites a **"Do Not Track"** request.

Location

- Lower down the **Privacy & Security** menu in the **Permissions** section there are options to allow or block requests to use your **Location**.

Block Pop-ups

- This option is listed as **Block pop-up windows** in the **Permissions** section of the **Privacy & Security** menu.

Dangerous Software and Websites

- The **Security** section at the bottom of the **Privacy & Security** menu states that Firefox will block dangerous or deceptive Web content and warn you if you've visited a **Deceptive Site** or an **Attack Site**. Also that Firefox protects you against *Phishing* and *Malware*, discussed elsewhere in this book.

Windows PC

Further Privacy Settings

Internet Explorer Browser

- Click the **Tools** gear icon shown on the right. Select **Internet Options** then **Privacy**.

Location

- Tick the box to block requests for your **Location**.

Block Pop-ups

- Tick the box to turn on the **Pop-up Blocker**.

Cookies

- Click **Advanced** shown above to accept or block first party and third party cookies.

First-party Cookies	Third-party Cookies
◉ Accept	◉ Accept
○ Block	○ Block
○ Prompt	○ Prompt
☐ Always allow session cookies	

Windows PC

Further Privacy Settings

Internet Explorer Browser (Continued from page 83)

Tracking Protection

- Click the **Tools** gear icon shown on the right and on page 83.
- Select **Safety** then **Turn on Tracking Protection**.
- Double-click **Your Personalised List**.
- Select either **Automatically block** or **Choose content to block or allow** as shown below.

> ⊘ Personalised Tracking Protection List
>
> When you visit multiple websites that contain content from the same provider, such as a map, advertisement or web measurement tools, some information about your visits might be shared with the content provider. If you choose to block content, portions of the websites you visit might not be available.
>
> ⦿ Automatically block   ○ Choose content to block or allow

Do Not Track

- Click the **Tools** gear icon shown above then select **Safety**.
- Select **Turn on Do Not Track** requests.
- Click the **Turn on** button and restart Internet Explorer.

Security

- Click the **Tools** gear icon shown above then select **Internet Options**.
- Click the **Security** tab. Move the blue slider up or down if you wish to change the security level from the default **Medium-high**. As this setting is intended to protect against malware and dangerous websites, it is obviously not a good idea to reduce the security level.

Windows PC
Further Privacy Settings
Microsoft Edge Browser

- Click the menu button shown on the right at the top right of the screen. Scroll down and select **Settings** and **View Advanced Settings.**

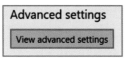

Block Pop-ups

- Click the button near the top of the **Advanced settings** panel to switch **Block pop-ups** On or Off.

Do Not Track

- Scroll down the **Advanced settings** panel and under **Privacy and services** click the button shown below to switch **Do Not Track** requests On or Off.

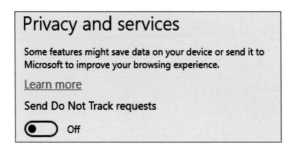

Windows PC

Further Privacy Settings

Microsoft Edge Browser
(Continued from page 85)

Cookies

- Scroll down the **Advanced settings** panel and under **Cookies** click **Don't block cookies**. This displays the three available options shown below.

> Block all cookies
>
> Block only third-party cookies
>
> Don't block cookies

Malicious Sites and Downloads

- At the bottom of the **Advanced settings** panel, make sure protection with **Windows Defender SmartScreen** is switched On as shown below.

> Keep me protected from malicious sites and downloads with Windows Defender SmartScreen.
>
> On

Location

- Click the Windows icon at the bottom left of the Windows screen then click the **Settings** gear icon shown on the right and click **Location**. Use the button shown below to allow or disallow the use of your **Location**.

> Location service
>
> On
>
> If an app is using your location, you'll see this icon: ⊙

Android Security

Introduction

Previous chapters discussed the privacy and security settings in *Web browsers* such as Chrome, Firefox, Safari, Internet Explorer and Microsoft Edge. Web browsers are *apps* or *programs*. If you don't like the default browser supplied with a new smartphone, tablet or other computer you can change it. For example, you can install Mozilla Firefox on an Android device, replacing the Google Chrome browser, provided by default on a new machine.

What is an Operating System?

The *Operating System (O.S.)* is quite different from a Web browser. The operating system has overall control of everything from saving and printing files or documents to executing programs such as Web browsers. Normally the operating system is pre-installed on a new computer.

A smartphone or tablet made by Samsung, Motorola, HTC, LG, or Sony, for example, has the Android (Google) operating system already installed. Similarly, all iPhones and iPads use the Apple iOS operating system and most PC computers use Microsoft Windows.

Google Android   Apple iOS   Microsoft Windows

Some companies, such as Samsung, tweak the standard Android O.S. produced by Google to include their own design changes.

Keeping Your O.S. Up-to-Date

Operating Systems are under constant development with new versions rolled out every year or so.

- Android started as Petite Four in 2009, followed by many versions such as KitKat, Marshmallow and Nougat until Oreo was launched in 2017.

- The Apple iOS operating system has progressed from iOS version 1 in 2007 to iOS 12 in 2018.

- Microsoft Windows 1 appeared in 1985 eventually leading to Windows 10 launching in 2015.

- The operating system is *updated* by downloading and installing *patches* to fix "bugs" or improve security.

- The operating system is *upgraded* by downloading and installing the latest version of the entire operating system, such as Android 8 Oreo, at the time of wrting. This should have "state-of-the-art" security.

However, if your device is several years old your device manufacturer such LG, HTC, Sony or Samsung may stop supporting your device with security patches or upgrades.

Also the latest version of an operating system may not be compatible with older smartphones, tablets and other computers. In that case you would need to buy a newer device to keep up-to-date.

O.S. Security Settings

There are many security settings within the three major operating systems, Android, iOS and Windows. The rest of this chapter discusses Android security settings. Similarly Chapter 9 covers iOS devices and Chapter 10 covers Windows machines.

Android Smartphones and Tablets
Android Security

Android is the operating system used on most of the world's smartphones and tablets. It is an example of *open-source software*. This means the program instructions, known as *source code*, are available for anyone to read and modify. So hackers can examine the software and find ways to exploit its weaknesses with malware and viruses.

Conversely the Apple iOS and Microsoft Windows operating systems are *closed-source* software and therefore harder for hackers and fraudsters to attack. However, there are many ways to keep an Android smartphone or tablet safe and secure, such as:

- Setting a *screen lock*.
- *Fingerprint* and *facial recognition*.
- *Encryption*.
- *Locking* the *SIM card* to prevent phone calls and text messages.
- Careful use of *passwords*.
- Only installing *apps*, i.e. software, from *trusted sources*.
- Installing *anti-virus* software.
- Installing *security patches* and the latest O.S.
- *Two-factor authentication*.
- Finding and locking a *lost* or *stolen phone* and erasing the data if the phone can't be recovered.

Android Smartphones and Tablets

Setting a Screen Lock

The screen lock is used to prevent other people from accessing your smartphone or tablet when it is first switched on or when you press the power button to awaken it from sleep mode.

- Tap the **Settings** icon shown on the right.
- Scroll down and under **Personal** tap **Security** shown below.

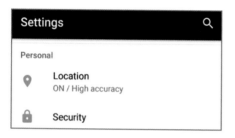

This opens the **Security** screen shown below.

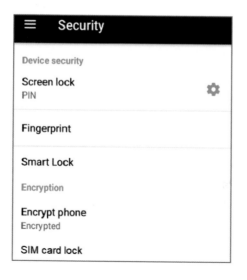

Android Smartphones and Tablets

- Tap **Screen lock** shown on the previous page, then choose your preferred method for unlocking the screen, as shown below.

None

Obviously **None** shown above offers no security at all. Anyone finding or stealing your phone would be able to switch on and start accessing your e-mails, and data, etc.

Using Swipe as a Screen Lock

The **Swipe** screen lock shown above requires you to swipe a padlock icon up the screen. With this setting the smartphone or tablet screen can easily be opened and accessed by anyone familiar with smartphones and tablets.

Using a Pattern as a Screen Lock

If you select **Pattern** shown above, you are warned that until the device starts up, it can't receive calls, messages or notifications including alarms. This helps protect data on lost or stolen phones.

Android Smartphones and Tablets

Using a Pattern as a Screen Lock
(Continued from page 91)

- Select **Pattern** shown on the previous page, then tap the option shown below.

- You are asked to choose your pattern by joining at least 4 dots by sliding with your finger, as shown in the example below.

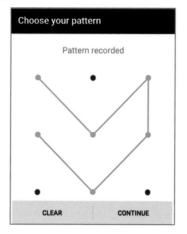

- Tap **CONTINUE** shown above and you are asked to draw the pattern again to confirm it.

- Tap **Confirm** to complete the setting up of the pattern as a screen lock.

- You will need to draw your chosen pattern by joining up white dots on a black screen every time you start your smartphone or tablet or wake it from sleep.

- You will also need to enter this pattern to change to another type of screenlock such as **PIN** or **Password**.

Android Smartphones and Tablets

Using a PIN as a Screen Lock

- Tap **Settings**, **Security** and **Screen lock** shown on page 90 to display the screen lock options shown again below.

- If you have already set another effective screen lock, e.g. a **Pattern** or a **Password**, you will need to enter this before you can display the screen lock options shown below.

← **Choose screen lock**

None
Current screen lock

Swipe

Pattern

PIN

Password

- Tap **PIN** shown above and having read the notice which appears, tap the option shown below.

 **Require PIN to start device**

You can then enter your **PIN**, as shown on the next page. which must contain at least 4 digits. A longer **PIN** is obviously safer and you should avoid unsafe ones such as **1234**, **1111**, **9999** or your birthday. The digits should be truly random.

Android Smartphones and Tablets

- After entering your **PIN** tap **CONTINUE** as shown above. You are then required to **Confirm your PIN** by re-entering it and tapping **OK**.
- Your screen lock is now set at **PIN**, as shown below.

Using a Password as a Screen Lock

- Tap **Screen lock** shown on page 90 and if necessary enter any previous **Pattern** or **Pin**. (Or a previous **Password** if you wish to change it).
- Tap **Password** as shown on page 93 and then tap the option shown below.

<table>
<tr><td>🔒</td><td>**Require password to start device**</td></tr>
</table>

- Enter a password as shown on the next page. The password should be at least 4 characters long, preferably more. Please see the notes on choosing a password in the top part of page 96

Android Smartphones and Tablets

- After entering your **Password** tap **CONTINUE** as shown above. You are then required to **Confirm your Password** by re-entering it and tapping **OK**.
- Your screen lock is now set at **Password**, as shown below.

Changing the Screen Lock

You can change the screen lock at any time, whether you are using a **Pattern**, **PIN** or **Password**. However, you will need to enter your current **Pattern**, **PIN** or **Password** before you can select a new screen lock as shown in the **Choose screen lock** menu on page 93.

Android Smartphones and Tablets

Password, PIN, or Pattern Screen Locks Compared

It's not a good idea to use as a Password your name, family or pets' names or places you are connected with. Many companies and websites recommend using at least 8 characters, including numbers and letters and upper and lower case letters. However, entering a long and complicated password on a phone is not really practical every time you start the device or wake it from sleep, perhaps many times a day.

Similarly, the Pattern has been found to be a weak form of security. This is because anyone nearby can see the pattern you enter and easily replicate it if they have access to your device.

The 4 or preferably 6-digit PIN is probably the most convenient screen lock, provided the numbers are truly random.

Setting a Fingerprint Screen Lock

This option appears on the main **Security** menu, opened as described on page 90.

- Select **Fingerprint** shown above to open the screen shown at the top of page 97.

Android Smartphones and Tablets

Unlock with fingerprint

Just touch the fingerprint sensor
to unlock your phone, authorise
purchases or sign in to apps. Be careful
whose fingerprints you add. Every print
added can do any of these things.

Note: your fingerprint may be less
secure than a strong pattern or PIN.
Find out more

@   Continue

- You are then told to locate the *Fingerprint sensor*, a button at the bottom of a smartphone, as shown below. Some more expensive tablets also have a Fingerprint sensor built into the Home button.

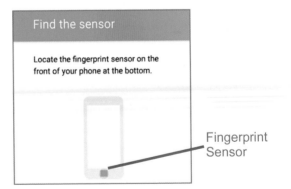

Find the sensor

Locate the fingerprint sensor on the
front of your phone at the bottom.

Fingerprint
Sensor

Once the set up is completed, as discussed on the next few pages, simply tap the Fingerprint sensor shown above whenever you need to unlock the smartphone (or one of those tablets equipped with a Fingerprint sensor).

Android Smartphones and Tablets

- Tap your finger a number of times on the sensor to record your Fingerprint.

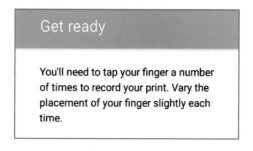

- As you keep tapping the sensor, an image of a Fingerprint gradually develops until your Fingerprint is saved on your device. This is indicated by the complete Fingerprint image shown below.

- Next tap **ADD ANOTHER** (Fingerprint) or select **NEXT** or **DONE** to finish.

Android Smartphones and Tablets

In the previous example, the phone already had a **PIN** screen lock. So the **Security** settings appeared as shown below.

Screen lock
PIN

Fingerprint
1 fingerprint set up

Set a Backup Screen Lock

The Fingerprint screen lock, while very fast and easy to use, is not as secure as a Pattern, Pin or Password. Therefore, you are advised to have a backup screen lock, in addition to Fingerprint. If you set up a Fingerprint screen lock on a new smartphone, you will see the following backup options. These can all be set up as just described.

Choose screen lock

Your fingerprint may be less secure than a strong pattern, PIN or password. For added security, set up a backup screen lock.

Fingerprint + Pattern

Fingerprint + PIN

Fingerprint + Password

Once set up you can unlock your phone or tablet by simply touching the fingerprint sensor shown on page 97.

Android Smartphones and Tablets

The Smart Lock

This is a feature which keeps your smartphone or tablet unlocked when it is safe to do so.

- Tap the **Settings** icon shown on the right and then select **Security** to open the menu shown below.

- Select **Smart Lock** shown above.

- You will be asked to confirm your current screen lock such as PIN, Password or Pattern.

- The **Smart Lock** menu appears, as shown on the next page.

Android Smartphones and Tablets

←	**Smart Lock**	⋮

🚶	**On-body detection** Keep your device unlocked while it's on you
📍	**Trusted places** Add location where device should be unlocked
🖳	**Trusted devices** Add device to keep this one unlocked when it's nearby
👤	**Trusted face** Set up facial recognition

On-body detection

- Tap this option shown above and switch it On. After you unlock the device it stays unlocked while you are holding or carrying it. It locks again when it is put down.

Trusted places

- Make sure **Location** is switched On as discussed on page 71. Select **Trusted places** shown above then tap **Add trusted place**. A map is displayed allowing you to select your current location as a place where it's safe to leave your device unlocked.

- Finally tap **Select this location** to add it to the list of **Trusted places**.

Android Smartphones and Tablets

The Smart Lock

(Continued)

Trusted devices

- *Bluetooth* is a wireless technology which allows devices such as smartphones and tablets to be connected over short distances (about 100 metres) for the exchange of data.

- The **Trusted devices** option in **Smart Lock** keeps the device unlocked while it is connected by Bluetooth to your other devices such as a Bluetooth watch or your car's Bluetooth. Tap **ADD TRUSTED DEVICE** to detect and connect to one of your Bluetooth devices.

Trusted face

- This option allows you to open a phone by facial recognition.

- Select the **Trusted face** option shown on page 101.

- You are warned that facial recognition is not as secure as a Pattern, PIN or Password.

- Someone who looks like you could unlock your phone.

- Tap **SET UP** to begin setting up facial recognition.

- Find a spot indoors that's not too bright or dim.

- Hold the phone at eye level.

- Tap **NEXT** and then **ALLOW** shown on the next page.

Android Smartphones and Tablets

Trusted face
(Continued)

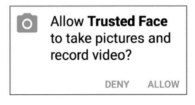

- Look at the screen so that your whole face is within the circle.

- Wait until the complete circle is white instead of red.

- You will see a tick and the message **Face added**.

- Tap **FINISHED** and you are now ready to unlock your phone by facial recognition.

- Tap **Trusted face** shown on page 101. There is now an option, as shown below, to **Improve face-matching**, by using different lighting, with or without prescription glasses, bearded or clean shaven and by holding the phone at eye level.

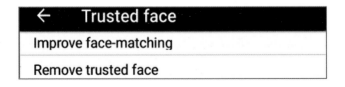

- To remove a face, select **Trusted face** shown on page 101 and select **Remove trusted face** as shown above.

Android Smartphones and Tablets

Encryption

This is essential to keep your data and personal information safe from thieves and hackers. **Encrypted** shown below scrambles the data on your phone (or tablet) so that it can only be decoded and read after entering your chosen screen lock, i.e. PIN, Password or Pattern.

Select **Security** as discussed on page 100 and scroll down to display the options shown below.

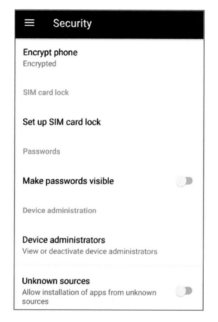

Encryption is normally switched on by default on later versions of Android. If not it can be switched On after tapping **Encrypt phone** (shown above) or **Encrypt tablet**. The process can take over an hour and requires the battery to be fully charged.

Android Smartphones and Tablets
SIM Card Lock

If you lock the SIM card, anyone stealing your phone can't use it to make phone calls unless they know the PIN provided by your cell phone network.

- Select **Set up SIM card lock** shown on page 104.

- Switch **Lock SIM card** On using the button shown on the right below.

- To use the **Change SIM PIN** option shown above, contact your cell phone network for a new PIN.

Apps from Unknown Sources

The Google Play Store is the main source for downloading new apps or programs. Apps in the Play Store should have been checked for malware, etc., before entering the store. However, you might download an app containing malware from a source other than the Google Play Store. To prevent this make sure **Unknown sources** shown below and on page 104 is switched Off, as shown below.

Android Smartphones and Tablets

2-Step Verification

This is an additional layer of security on top of the Username and Password, PIN or Pattern screen lock discussed earlier.

Also known as Two Factor Authentication (2FA), it is intended to guard against people who may know your PIN or Password, etc.

After entering your username and password, a 6 digit, automatically generated, one-time only verification code is sent to your phone as an SMS text message or phone call.

Turning on 2-Step Verification on Your Google Account

Your Google Account, created during the setting up of a new Android device, is used for many of the services on Android smartphones and tablets. Apart from all the apps such as Gmail, Google Drive (cloud storage), etc., it is used to sync all your photos, documents, etc., and folders between all the devices you are signed into. Open your Web browser such as Google Chrome.

- Search for **google account**.
- Select **Sign-in & security**.
- Scroll down and tap **2-step Verification**
- Tap **GET STARTED** and follow the instructions on the screen.
- Tap **TURN ON** next to **2-Step Verification**.
- Make sure the number is correct for the phone you wish to receive the verification codes on.
- The 2-Step Verification is tested by sending a verification code to your phone.

Android Smartphones and Tablets

Forgetting Your Password, Pattern or PIN

If you can't remember your Password, PIN or Pattern, used to unlock your phone or tablet, you can you can re-set it if you know your Google e-mail address and the password for your Google Account.

On another computer, laptop, tablet, sign in to your Google account.

- Search for **google account** in a Web browser such as Google Chrome.

- Select **Sign-in & security**.

- Under **Find your phone**, tap **GET STARTED**.

- Select the smartphone, or tablet, etc. you wish to reset. (If you are signed in to Google on more than one device you will see a list of devices).

- Enter the password for your Google Account.

- Select **Lock your phone**.

- Enter a new password to lock the screen.

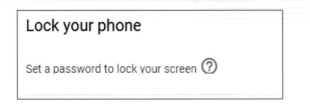

- You should now be able to unlock your phone or tablet with the new password created on the other computer, laptop or tablet.

Android Smartphones and Tablets

Lost or Stolen Phones

If your smartphone is lost or stolen there several steps to either find and retrieve the phone or protect your data.

- On another computer, etc., open **Find your phone** as described on page 107.
- Select the device you wish to find and enter the password for your Google Account.
- On the **Find your phone** screen, there are several options, as listed below.
- Call your phone if you think it may be lost within your earshot or found by a person who may return it to you. Ring
- Show where the phone is on a map using Locate. **Locate**.
- **Lock your phone** so a thief can't access the data.
- **Consider erasing your device**.
- Ask the person holding the phone to call you.

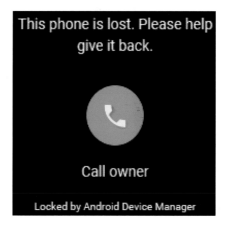

This phone is lost. Please help give it back.

Call owner

Locked by Android Device Manager

Android Smartphones and Tablets
Keeping Android Up-to-Date

As mentioned earlier, it's most important that you keep your Android operating sytem updated with the latest security software. This can be done in two ways:

- If possible, *upgrading* to the latest version of the Android operating system.

- Downloading the latest *security patches* or *updates* to the operating system, which are released regularly.

Versions of Android

The Android operating system has evolved over many versions. As of May 2018, the installed user base of the most recent and heavily used versions was as follows:

Launched	Version	User Base
2013	4.4 KitKat	10%
2014	5 Lollipop	22%
2015	6 Marshmallow	26%
2016	7 Nougat	31%
2017	6 Oreo	6%

Generally, if you have a phone or tablet made in the last two years, you should be able to upgrade to the latest version. However, this depends on the manufacturer, such as Samsung or Motorola, etc. At the time of writing in July 2018, Oreo is still not available as an upgrade to Nougat, on some devices. Some early machines won't ever receive a new version. In that case, the only way to keep up-to-date is to buy a new smartphone or tablet.

Android Smartphones and Tablets
Installing Updates

New versions of the operating system and security patches can be downloaded and installed as follows:

- Make sure the device is connected to Wi-Fi.
- Tap the **Settings** icon shown on the right.
- Scroll down and tap **About phone** or **About tablet**.
- Select **System updates** near the top of the next screen.
- Android will check for any updates.
- If updates are available, tap to download and **Install** them. Alternatively you will be told that your software is up-to-date.
- On some Samsung phones and tablets tap **About device** to switch on **Download update automatically**.

Third Party Security Software

Installing third party anti-virus and security software from Norton, McAfee, etc., is discussed in Chapter 11.

iOS Security

Introduction

It is often reported that the iOS operating system used in Apple smartphones and tablets is more secure than the Android operating system discussed in Chapter 8. Both systems are extremely popular, selling many millions of copies worldwide. While Apple iPhones and iPads using iOS are the most popular individual brands, Android devices dominate numerically because they are made by numerous very large companies such as LG, Samsung, Sony, Motorola, etc., etc.

Apple iOS devices such as the iPhone and iPad are considered to be more secure than Androids because:

- Apple doesn't release the *source code*, i.e. program instructions for iOS, making it harder for a fraudster to write malware, etc.

- This contrasts with Android's *open-source* operating system which can be tweaked or modified by anyone, giving rise to security risks.

- Apple keeps tight control of new software entering the App Store. Android's open-source software allows new apps to be easily written, including malware, phishing and adware, etc.

- When Apple releases an upgrade to iOS, including "bug" fixes and security patches, everyone gets it very quickly. It takes a long time for the latest version of Android to reach a large user base.

iPhones and iPads

iOS Security Settings

The following settings are built into the iOS operating system:

- Setting a *Passcode* or screen lock.
- Setting *Auto-lock*.
- A *Require a Passcode* option.
- Your *Apple ID* and *Two-factor authentication*.
- Fingerprint and facial recognition. (If available).
- Encryption.
- Locking the SIM card to prevent other people making phone calls and sending text messages.
- Installing security patches and the latest O.S.
- Finding a locked or stolen phone.
- Erasing data.

The Passcode

The Passcode is essential to stop unauthorised access to your smartphone or tablet when the device starts up, when it has been locked when not used for a while, or before you change settings. The Passcode should be turned on by default but if not:

- Select the **Settings** icon shown on the right and then tap **Touch ID & Passcode**.
- Tap Turn Passcode On as shown below.

Touch ID & Passcode	Turn Passcode On

iPhones and iPads
4-digit or 6-digit Passcodes

Later versions of iOS require a 6-digit Passcode. You will need to create this when you set up a new phone or tablet. Earlier devices used a 4-digit Passcode. In the event of a fraudster trying to guess your Passcode, the 4-digit code has 10,000 possible combinations. The 6-digit code is more secure, with a possible 1,000,000 codes.

If you find a 6-digit code too laborious to keep entering at regular intervals you can re-set it to the less secure 4 digits or even set an *alphanumeric code*. These options are discussed shortly.

On starting up your device or waking it up from sleep, you will be required to enter your 4-digit or 6-digit Passcode, as shown below.

iPhones and iPads

Setting Auto-Lock

This is used to prevent unauthorised access to a smartphone or tablet, if you leave it where other people may see it. If the device is unused for a certain time, the screen goes blank and the tablet is locked. The device can also be locked by tapping the power button. It is unlocked by entering your Passcode and can then be used again.

- Tap the **Settings** icon shown on the right.

- Tap **Display & Brightness** on the left-hand side of the **Settings** screen shown below.

- Tap **Auto-Lock** on the right-hand side of the **Settings** screen to open the **Auto-Lock** time options shown below.

iPad 🛜	10:45
Settings	‹ Display & Brightness **Auto-Lock**
📶 Bluetooth	Off
	2 Minutes
🔔 Notifications	5 Minutes
🎛 Control Centre	10 Minutes
🌙 Do Not Disturb	15 Minutes
⚙️ General ①	Never
AA Display & Brightness	

As shown above, setting the phone or tablet to lock after only **2 Minutes** is the most secure option, while **Never** is obviously extremely risky.

iPhones and iPads

Requiring a Passcode

When you start a smartphone or tablet you must enter a Passcode to unlock it. After that you may need to re-enter the Passcode every time the screen goes black and the phone is auto-locked. To prevent this you can set a time during which the Passcode will not need to be re-entered.

- Select **Settings**, as described on page 114, then tap **Touch ID & Passcode** as shown below.

- Now tap **Require Passcode** in the right-hand panel and select a time period during which a Passcode <u>will not be needed</u>, as shown below.

Settings		‹ Touch ID & Passcode **Require Passcode**
⚙ General	①	Immediately ✓
AA Display & Brightness		After 1 minute
✳ Wallpaper		After 5 minutes
🔊 Sounds		After 15 minutes
Siri & Search		After 1 hour
👆 Touch ID & Passcode		After 4 hours
		Shorter times are more secure.

The default time **Immediately** shown above is the most secure, meaning a Passcode is needed whenever you try to unlock the phone. The least secure option is **After 4 hours**, shown above. This allows you to use the phone for 4 hours before a Passcode is required.

iPhones and iPads

Changing Your Passcode

You can change your Passcode at any time, *as long as you know the current code*, which you are required to enter and confirm at several stages during the process.

- Open **Settings** as described on page 114 and select **Touch ID & Passcode** in the left-hand panel as shown on page 115.
- Enter your Passcode in the window shown below.

- Select **Change Passcode** in the right-hand panel of the **Settings** screen, as shown below.

iPhones and iPads

- The **Change Passcode** window opens, as shown below.

- To change your Passcode to a new one but in the same format as the current one, enter and confirm the new Passcode in the window as shown above.

- To set up a new Passcode in a different format, tap **Passcode Options** shown above to display the options shown below.

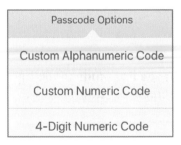

You can then enter and confirm a Passcode in one of the formats shown above. **Alphanumeric** is a mixture of letters and digits, **Custom Numeric** is the 6-digit Passcode.

4-digits is the earlier, less secure default iOS Passcode.

iPhones and iPads

Erase Data

If someone enters the wrong Passcode ten times, the **Erase Data** option wipes all of the data on the smartphone or tablet. You might want to switch **Erase Data** on to protect your data if the smartphone or tablet is stolen.

Please Note: Use Erase Data With Caution

However, to use this option you should have already backed up your data in the clouds, as discussed in Chapter 12. Otherwise you would lose everything, personal information, irreplaceable photos, etc., etc. iTunes can be used to restore your backed up data and also reset your Passcode if you forget it.

- Open **Settings** as described on page 114 and select **Touch ID & Passcode** in the left-hand panel as shown on page 115 and shown below.

- Scroll down to see **Erase Data** shown below in the off setting. Tap the button shown on the right below.

- The following warning appears:

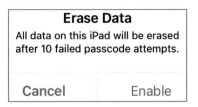

Tap Enable shown above to switch **Erase Data** on, indicated by the button, now partly green, shown below.

iPhones and iPads

Encryption

Under **Erase Data** on the right-hand of the **Settings** screen, as discussed on page 118, the message **Data protection is enabled** should be displayed as shown below.

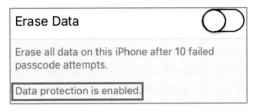

The message **Data protection is enabled** means the data saved on your smartphone or tablet is *encrypted*, i.e. scrambled so that it's unreadable by a hacker, thief or fraudster, without first being *decrypted*. This requires the use of your Passcode. For maximum security you should set **Require Passcode** discussed on page 115 to **Immediately** and set a 6-digit or alphanumeric Passcode, as discussed earlier in this chapter. Once you've set a Passcode, encryption and data protection are set up on your device.

If you tap **Turn Passcode Off** in **Settings** as shown below and discussed on page 112, the message **Data protection is enabled** will not appear as shown above.

| Touch ID & Passcode | Turn Passcode Off |

Turn Passcode On and Set a Strong Passcode

Apart from unlocking your device, the Passcode is essential in encrypting and decrypting your data. Without a Passcode you are at much greater risk of your data and your money being stolen.

iPhones and iPads

Touch ID

This feature is available on later iPhones and iPads starting with the iPhone 5S in 2013. A fingerprint scanner in the Home button allows you to quickly unlock the device with your finger and to make purchases from the App Store.

- Make sure you have a working Passcode.

- Open **Settings** as described on page 114 and select **Touch ID & Passcode** in the left-hand panel as shown below. (If available).

- Enter your Passcode as shown on page 116.

- Select Add a Fingerprint on the right of the **Settings** screen, as shown below.

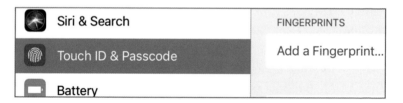

- You are told to **Lift and rest your finger on the Home button repeatedly**. Do not click the Home button, just rest your finger on it.

- You are repeatedly instructed to **Lift Your Finger**, then **Place Your Finger**, changing the position of your finger each time.

- After lifting and placing your finger on the Home button several times, **Touch ID** or fingerprint recognition should be set up on your smartphone or tablet, as shown on the next page.

iPhones and iPads

Complete

Touch ID is ready. Your print can be used for unlocking your iPad.

Continue

Now your finger can be used to unlock the smartphone or tablet – there's no need to enter your Passcode. (Although you still need a Passcode, e.g. to change settings). The fingerprint, **Finger 1**, shown below can now be used for the services switched on in green below. Additional finger prints can be added and used to unlock the device.

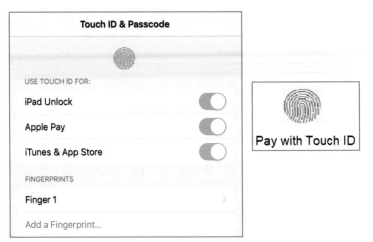

Touch ID & Passcode

USE TOUCH ID FOR:

iPad Unlock

Apple Pay

iTunes & App Store

FINGERPRINTS

Finger 1

Add a Fingerprint...

Pay with Touch ID

iPhones and iPads

Face ID

Facial recognition was introduced in 2017 on the iPhone X and is not yet widely available on other iOS devices. iPhone 11, iPhone 12 and the more affordable IPhone 9 are due to be released soon and will also have Face ID. As they will have no Home button, Touch ID will not be available.

Face ID provides an easy way to unlock the phone and to make payments for purchases from the App Store, iTunes and using Apple Pay. Apple say it is much more secure than Touch ID unless you have an "evil identical twin".

Setting Up Face ID

- Open the **Settings** screen as discussed on page 114.
- Select **Face ID & Password** (if available).
- Enter your Passcode if required.
- Tap **Set Up Face ID**.
- Tap **Get Started**.
- Look into your phone and move your head within the circle displayed on the screen. This should complete the circle with small radial lines on its circumference.
- Tap **Continue**.
- Move your head to complete the circle a second time.
- Tap **Done**.

Using Face ID

- Tap the Home button to wake up the phone.
- Glance at the Phone.
- When the padlock icon changes to open, swipe up from the bottom to unlock the phone.

iPhones and iPads
Your Apple ID

This consists of a *User Name* and a *Password*. The User Name should be a valid e-mail address as shown below.

User Name: stellajohnson99@gmail.com
Password: RadBourne47

Your Apple ID is created during the setting up of a new iPad or iPhone and saved on your device, so you don't need to keep entering it. An Apple ID can also be created when you sign in to iCloud and iTunes for the first time.

Your account for everything Apple.

A single Apple ID and password gives you access to
all Apple services. Learn more about Apple ID ›

Secure Password

The Password should have at least eight characters and include upper and lower case letters and one or more numbers. The Apple ID Password is not to be confused with the 4-digit, 6-digit or alphanumeric Passcode used to unlock your screen, as discussed earlier in this chapter.

Anyone who knows the User Name and Password for your Apple ID could access your data and photos, etc., *on any computer*. They simply enter **iCloud.com** into a Web browser and sign in with your Apple ID. To prevent this, use *Two-Factor Authentication*, as discussed on the next page. This provides an extra layer of security for your data.

iPhones and iPads

Two-Factor Authentication

If a fraudster obtains your Apple ID, they can access your data on any computer, smartphone or tablet. Two-Factor Authentication prevents this by requiring the entry of a *6-digit Verification Code* sent to a *Trusted Device*, such as an iPhone which only you have access to.

Setting Up Two-Factor Authentication

- Open **Settings** as described on page 114.
- Tap your name at the top left of **Settings**.
- Tap **Password & Security**.
- Tap **Turn On Two-Factor Authentication**.
- Tap **Continue.**
- Enter the trusted phone number you wish to receive the verification code by text message or phone call.
- Tap **Next**. Apple sends a verification code to the trusted device, i.e. phone.
- Enter the verification code to turn on **Two-Factor Authentication** as shown below.

Two-Factor Authentication	On

Your trusted devices and phone numbers are used to verify your identity when signing in.

TRUSTED PHONE NUMBER	Edit

+44 7539 480

Trusted phone numbers are used to verify your identity when signing in and to help recover your account if you have forgotten your password.

Get Verification Code

Get a verification code to sign in on another device or at iCloud.com.

iPhones and iPads

Using Two-Factor Authentication

iCloud is the Apple Internet storage system, as discussed in Chapter 12, where all your documents, photos, etc., should be securely backed up. The example below shows how to sign in to iCloud on a Windows PC to view data backed up from an iPad. Two-Factor Authentication on the iPad stops anyone else from doing this on another computer.

- Enter **iCloud.com** in a browser such as Chrome on any computer.

- Select **Sign in to iCloud – Apple.** Enter your Apple ID.

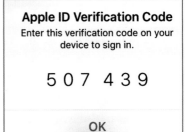

- A one-time verification code, as shown above on the right, is sent to your trusted device (Such as an iPhone). Enter the verification code to finish signing in to iCloud.

iPhones and iPads

Resetting Your Password

This is the Password used with your e-mail address to make up your Apple ID, as shown on page 123. It is not the same as your 4-digit, 6-digit or alphanumeric screen lock Passcode discussed on page 113. The Password will normally be permanently saved on your smartphone or tablet, but you might need to create a new one, if you think someone may know the old one or you have forgotten it. You may need to enter your Passcode several times during the process.

Two-Factor Authentication should be On as discussed on page 124.

- Open **Settings** as shown on page 114.
- Tap your name at the top left-hand side of the screen.
- Tap **Password & Security**.

 ❮ Apple ID   **Password & Security**

 Change Password

 Two-Factor Authentication

 Your trusted devices and phone numbers are used to verify your identity when signing in.

 TRUSTED PHONE NUMBER

- Tap Change Password shown above.
- Enter your iPad Passcode.
- Enter the **New** Password, then enter the password again to **Verify** it. (At least 8 characters, with upper and lower case letters and at least one number).

iPhones and iPads

The following note appears:

> ### Sign out other devices using your Apple ID?
>
> If you think someone might know your password, you can force all devices and websites using your Apple ID to sign out.
>
> Sign Out Other Devices

- Select **Sign Out Other Devices** shown above to require your new Apple ID Password to be entered to access your data on other devices. The word **Changing** appears and the password is very quickly changed.

Forgetting Your Screen Lock Passcode

This is the 4-digit, 6-digit or alphanumeric Passcode used to unlock the screen on an iPhone or iPad. If you forget the Passcode or someone enters the wrong Passcode 10 times you may need to wipe your device and start again with a new Passcode. This will happen automatically if you have set **Erase Data** On, as discussed on page 118.

To restore your data you need to have made a backup copy of your device to iTunes on another computer before erasing and then restoring the data. This is a complex task and you might need to entrust the work to an Apple Retail Store or Apple Authorised Service Provider.

> To avoid this major task of erasing and restoring your data and Passcode, use a secure Passcode which you can easily remember but no-one else can deduce from your personal details. Or write it down in a very secure place.

iPhones and iPads

Find My Phone

This is used to find a lost or stolen iPhone (or an iPad with Wi-Fi or 3G/4G cell phone connectivity).

- Install the **Find iPhone** app from the App Store and tap the icon. Or enter **iCloud.com** into a browser, such as Google Chrome, on any device and sign in with your Apple ID, if necessary.

- Tap **All Devices** and select the one you want to find, as shown below on the left.

- A map is displayed showing the Location of your device and a window, shown on the right below.

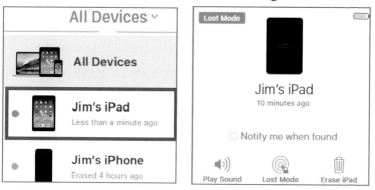

- **Lost Mode** on the right above is used to enter messages on the device or get e-mails of its Location.

- **Erase iPad** can be used to wipe your phone to stop a thief accessing the data on your iPhone or iPad.

Unless you set up Two-Factor Authentication, discussed on pages 124 and 125, anyone who knows your Apple ID can track your Location. (If **Find iPhone** is switched on in **Settings > Privacy > Location Services**).

iPhones and iPads

Using a SIM PIN to Protect Your Phone

A SIM card connects a smartphone to a network such as EE, O2, etc. You can set a *PIN (Personal Identification Number)* which must be entered before anyone can use the phone. If you forget the **PIN** you must enter a *PUK (Personal Unlocking Key)* to reset a **PIN**. The default **PIN** and the **PUK** number may be printed on the packaging of a new SIM card, as shown below. Otherwise contact your cell phone network provider. **1111** is the default **PIN** for the EE network.

Switching the SIM PIN On or Off

- Enter **Settings** as shown on page 114, then tap **Phone** and **SIM PIN**.

- Tap the switch shown below to switch **SIM PIN** on or off.

- Enter the default or current **SIM PIN** and tap **Done**.

Changing the SIM PIN

- Tap **Change PIN** shown above and enter the default or current **PIN** and tap **Done**.

- Enter and confirm the new **PIN** and tap **Done**.

iPhones and iPads

Updating and Upgrading iOS

Apple regularly issues updates to fix "bugs", improve security or upgrades to the latest version of iOS.

- You should be notified when updates and upgrades are available.

- Or tap **Settings**, shown on the right and select **General** and **Software Update**, shown below, to view any available updates

⚙ General	Software Update

- Any updates appear as shown below.

‹ General   **Software Update**

iOS 11.4.1
Apple Inc.
203.8 MB

iOS 11.4.1 includes bug fixes and improves the security of your iPhone or iPad. This update:

- Fixes an issue that prevented some users from viewing the last known location of their AirPods in Find My iPhone

- Tap **Download and Install** to update your device.

- Ideally, for maximum security, you should regularly see a similar note to the following whenever you tap **Software Update** in **Settings** > **General** shown above.

iOS 11.4.1
Your software is up to date.

Windows Security

Introduction

Microsoft Windows has been the dominant operating system on laptop and desktop computers for many years. The latest version is Windows 10, but many people are still using earlier versions such as Windows XP and Windows 7. Windows 10 Mobile is available for Windows Phones and smaller tablets.

Security Updates

Microsoft regularly issues security updates and it's important that these are downloaded and installed as soon as possible. Windows 10 downloads and installs updates automatically, whereas this was optional in earlier versions. Some people neglected to install security patches even when they were available.

What's new

Lucky you! Your device just got the latest Windows 10 update with new features and important security updates. Find out what's new and get suggestions for using Windows Tips.

Windows Desktops, Laptops and Tablets

Older Versions Are Less Secure

For maximum security you should try to update to the latest version of Windows whenever possible. In 2017 there were serious problems in some large organisations still using Windows XP, first released in 2001.

Microsoft stopped supporting Windows XP in 2014 and therefore it does not receive the latest security updates. A piece of malware called *WannaCry* was able to infect many thousands of computers worldwide and cause massive disruptions. These included large organisations still running Windows XP. Security patches developed by Microsoft to defend against WannaCry were not available for Windows XP. WannaCry is an example of *ransomware*, a piece of malware which locks the files on your computer by encryption. To decrypt the files with a key held only by the fraudster, you must agree to pay a ransom, using *Bitcoin*, a form of digital *cryptocurrency* payable across the Internet.

Windows Security Settings

Microsoft Windows is the operating system used by many large organisations as well as millions of individual users. So it's not surprising that it has lots of built-in updating and security features. To view these settings select the Windows **Start** icon, shown on the right, at the bottom left of the screen.

Now select the **Settings** gear icon, shown on the right.

This opens the **Windows Settings** screen, shown on the next page.

Windows Desktops, Laptops and Tablets

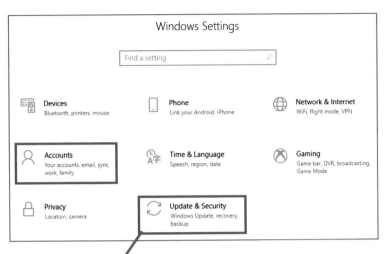

Select **Update & Security** shown above to open the **Update & Security** window shown below.

Select **Windows Update** shown below on the left, to see if your system is up to date. Alternatively select **Check for updates**.

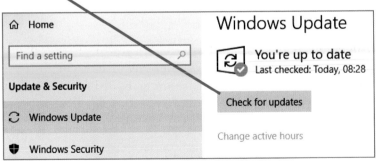

Windows Update is discussed in more detail later in this chapter.

Windows Desktops, Laptops and Tablets

Select **Windows Security** shown near the bottom of page 133 to see the list of security features shown below.

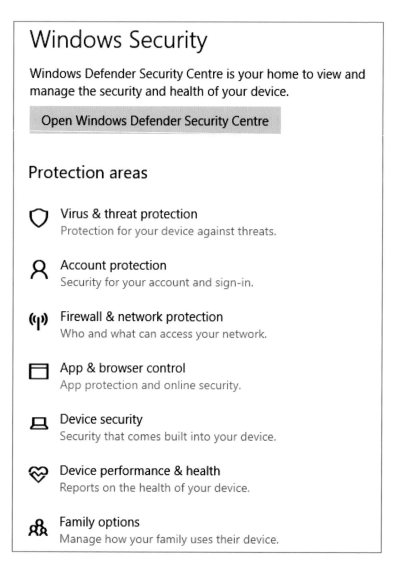

Windows Security

Windows Defender Security Centre is your home to view and manage the security and health of your device.

Open Windows Defender Security Centre

Protection areas

Virus & threat protection
Protection for your device against threats.

Account protection
Security for your account and sign-in.

Firewall & network protection
Who and what can access your network.

App & browser control
App protection and online security.

Device security
Security that comes built into your device.

Device performance & health
Reports on the health of your device.

Family options
Manage how your family uses their device.

Windows Desktops, Laptops and Tablets

Select **Open Windows Defender Security Centre** shown on page 134 to see a review of the security of your system as shown below in **Security at a glance**.

The ticks above indicate that no remedial action is needed on most security settings, on this computer on this occasion. However, the cross on the right and above shows that **Firewall & network protection** is turned off. This can be corrected using the **Turn on** button shown on the right and above.

The **Firewall** and other topics listed above and under **Protection areas** on page 134 are discussed in more detail on the pages which follow.

Windows Desktops, Laptops and Tablets

Virus and Threat Protection

Viruses are malicious programs designed to damage your files and data and cause inconvenience. Viruses in one device can spread and infect other smartphones, tablets and larger computers. Many third-party companies develop anti-virus software and this subject is discussed in Chapter 11. Windows 10 has its own built-in *Windows Defender Antivirus* software which scans for viruses. This employs the latest *virus definitions*, used to recognise new viruses as they appear.

Select **Virus & threat protection** shown on page 134 to open the screen shown below.

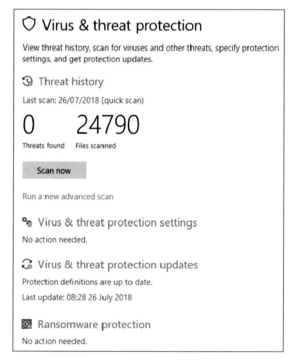

Windows Desktops, Laptops and Tablets

As shown on the previous page, **Virus & threat protection** displays the **Threat history** and the number of files scanned. Select **Scan now** to carry out an immediate scan.

If you select **Virus & threat protection settings** shown on page 136, you can make sure **Real-time protection** is switched **On**, as shown below, to stop malware running on your device.

Real-time protection

Locates and stops malware from installing or running on your device. You can turn off this setting for a short time before it turns back on automatically.

🔘 On

Virus & threat protection updates on page 136 allows you to check for and install the latest virus definition files.

Ransomware protection on page 136 allows you to select folders to be protected against criminals who encrypt, i.e. encode, your data so that you can no longer access it. Then they demand a payment to decrypt your data with a *key*, which they hold, so that you can use your data again.

 # Ransomware protection

Protect your files against threats such as ransomware and see how to restore files in case of an attack.

Controlled folder access

Protect files, folders and memory areas on your device from unauthorised changes by unfriendly apps.

🔘 On

Windows Desktops, Laptops and Tablets

Account Protection

Select **Account protection**, shown on page 134, to display the following:

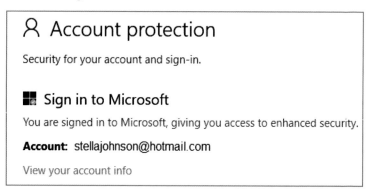

Sign in to Microsoft shown above allows you to add a photo to your account, so you can quickly see if you are signed in. **View your account info** shown above displays options shown on the left below. **Your info** includes details of your Microsoft payments and bills. **Email & app accounts** lists the accounts on your machine and allows you to add, delete and manage accounts. **Sign-in options** are discussed on the next page.

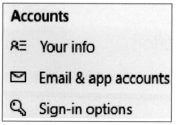

The menu on the left above can also be accessed by selecting **Start > Settings > Accounts** as shown above on the right and on page 133 on the **Windows Settings** screen.

Windows Desktops, Laptops and Tablets

Sign-in Options

If you select **Sign-in options**, shown at the bottom of page 138, several alternatives are displayed, as shown below.

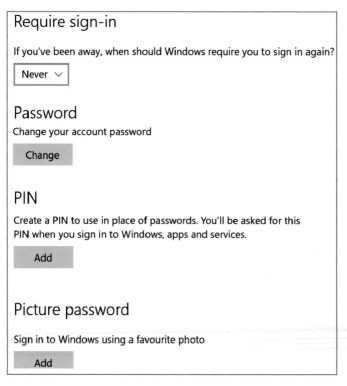

Require sign-in

If you've been away, when should Windows require you to sign in again?

Never ∨

Password
Change your account password

Change

PIN

Create a PIN to use in place of passwords. You'll be asked for this PIN when you sign in to Windows, apps and services.

Add

Picture password

Sign in to Windows using a favourite photo

Add

The above settings are discussed on the next few pages.

Some of the latest Windows devices have additional options for signing in, which don't require a **Password** or a **PIN**. These options, known as **Windows Hello**, recognise your physical features such as your fingerprints or face, as discussed on page 142.

Windows Desktops, Laptops and Tablets

Sign-in Options (Continued)

Require sign-in

Your computer will go to "sleep" after a pre-set time, (from 1 minute to 2 hours) if it's switched on but not being used. This time is set in **Settings** > **System** > **Power & sleep**.

When you wake up the device by clicking with the mouse or double-tapping the screen, etc., you can require a sign-in. **Never** shown below is very insecure if you leave your machine "sleeping" where other people have access to it.

> ### Require sign-in
>
> If you've been away, when should Windows require you to sign in again?
>
> Never
>
> When PC wakes up from sleep

Password

This option, shown on page 139, allows you to **Create** and **Re-enter** to confirm a new password after first entering your current password, as shown below.

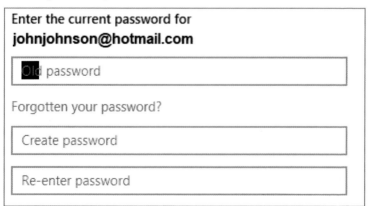

> **Enter the current password for**
> **johnjohnson@hotmail.com**
>
> Old password
>
> Forgotten your password?
>
> Create password
>
> Re-enter password

Windows Desktops, Laptops and Tablets

Setting a PIN

Instead of a password, you can sign into Windows using a **PIN** after selecting **Add** shown below and on page 139.

The **PIN** must have at least 4 digits. The more digits in a **PIN**, the more secure it is, but also the harder it is to remember. Obvious **PINs** such as 1234 should be avoided.

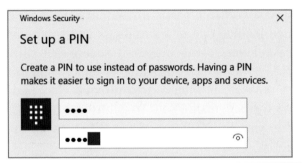

The **PIN** supplements, rather than replaces, the Password, on the machine it is set up on. It gives a quick and easy way to sign in when you start the device or when it wakes from sleep. The **PIN** is *local*, i.e. it only applies to the machine it is set up on.

Someone who knows your Microsoft User ID and password could access your data on any machine running Microsoft Windows. If someone knows your **PIN** but not your password, they can only access your data using the computer on which you set up the **PIN**.

Sign-in Options (Continued)

Picture Password

This sign-in option listed on page 139 is available on touchscreen devices and requires you to select a photo to use as the picture password. The password is created by drawing on the picture with your finger, using three gestures which can be circles, dots or straightlines. The device is unlocked by repeating the gestures in the correct positions on the picture.

Windows Hello

Signing in using a password or PIN can be very frustrating, especially if you have a lot of different accounts with different passwords. A password should have eight or more characters, include one or more digits and some upper and lower case letters. This makes it secure but difficult to remember. *Windows Hello* available under **Sign-in options** on some devices, is intended to provide easy and secure signing in by recognising your fingerprints or face.

Sign-in options

Require sign-in

If you've been away, when should Windows require you to sign in again?

| Never ∨ |

☺ Windows Hello

Sign in to Windows, apps and services by teaching Windows to recognise you.

Devices which do not have built-in face and fingerprint technology may be able to use *companion devices* such as Microsoft Band and some Windows phones.

Windows Desktops, Laptops and Tablets

Two-Step Verification

As discussed elsewhere in this book, Two-Step or Two-Factor authentication provides another layer of security after you enter your Microsoft Account password. A security code is then sent to a separate location that only you can access. This might be a phone or an e-mail address. So even if someone finds your password they will not be able to access your Microsoft Account and your files.

Setting Up Two-Step Verification

- Open the **Windows Settings** screen as discussed on pages 132 and 133.
- Select **Accounts > Your info > Manage my Microsoft account**.
- Select **Security**.
- Under **Security basics** select more security options.

> Explore more security options to help keep your account secure.

- Under **Additional security options**, select Set up two-step verification shown below.

Two-step verification

Two-step verification is an advanced security feature

Set up two-step verification

- Then follow the instructions on the screen.

Windows Desktops, Laptops and Tablets

Firewall and Network Protection

The Windows Defender Firewall is a piece of software designed to protect your computer from hackers and malware (malicious software). Windows Defender Firewall should be turned on in Windows Settings, as discussed on page 135. Select **Firewall & network protection** shown on page 134.

((ı)) Firewall & network protection
Who and what can access your network.

The window shown below opens, stating that the Firewall is switched On for three different types of network, **Domain**, **Private** and **Public**. Windows Defender Firewall has a group of settings for each type of network. When you sign into a new network, you are asked to set the network as Private or Public, as discussed on page 145 and 146.

((ı)) Firewall & network protection

View network connections, specify Windows Defender Firewall settings and troubleshoot network and Internet problems.

▦ Domain network

Firewall is on.

♀ Private network (active)

Firewall is on.

▭ Public network

Firewall is on.

Windows Desktops, Laptops and Tablets

Types of Network
Domain Networks

A *domain* in general is an area under one rule. A *domain network* is a group of computers in an organisation such as a large company or college, etc. Each client computer is connected to a central, secure server computer called a *domain controller*. This should be a very secure network as it's managed by a network administrator, so there should be control over apps, passwords and Internet connections.

Most individual users will use either Private or Public networks and these are the optional settings when connecting to a new network, as shown on page 146.

Private Networks

This might be your home-based or small business network connected to a router, for example, where you might share files with other computers and print documents. Your computer is "discoverable", so people you trust can connect to your computer and see what you're doing. The Public Firewall settings need to be more restrictive than the Private Firewall settings. A Home network is normally protected by a password on the router.

Public Networks

These are networks in cafés, airports and other public places. When a network is set to Public, Windows prevents other computers from connecting to your computer and accessing your files, etc. These are the least secure networks and should be used with caution.

If you are connecting to a network in a public place you should make sure it is set to Public, so that Windows Firewall can use the most restrictive or secure controls.

Windows Desktops, Laptops and Tablets

Setting a Network as Public or Private

You can set a network to **Private** or **Public** when connecting to the network for the first time, as shown below.

- Select the Wi-Fi icon on the Taskbar at the bottom right of the screen, shown on the right.
- Select the network from the list and select **Connect**.
- Enter the network password and select **Next**.
- Select **Yes** or **No** as shown below.

- To set it as a private network where your PC will be discoverable to other devices on the network, choose **Yes**.

- To set it as a public network where your PC won't be discoverable to other devices on the network, choose **No**.

Changing Existing Public or Private Settings

- To change the network type select the Wi-Fi icon shown on the right and select **Properties**.

- To use the most restrictive and secure Firewall settings make sure **Public** is On, as shown below.

- Otherwise switch on the less secure **Private** setting shown below if you trust the network and its users. **Private** will allow several devices on the same network to share files and to print.

⦿ Public

Your PC is hidden from other devices on the network and can't be used for printer and file sharing.

◯ Private

For a network you trust, such as at home or work. Your PC is discoverable and can be used for printer and file sharing if you set it up.

Windows Desktops, Laptops and Tablets

Virtual Private Networks

A VPN allows you to connect securely to the Internet, even if your computer is using a free public Wi-Fi network. You connect to the Internet via a *VPN server*, **belonging to a** *VPN provider* **and this** server may be in another country. While you use the Internet your identity is hidden from potential hackers. Virtual Private Networks are discussed in more detail in Chapter 11.

More Windows Security Protection Areas

Some more **Protection areas** listed on page 134 are discussed on the next few pages and for convenience are shown again highlighted in the extract below.

Protection areas

🛡 Virus & threat protection
Protection for your device against threats.

🧑 Account protection
Security for your account and sign-in.

((•)) Firewall & network protection
Who and what can access your network.

🖥 App & browser control
App protection and online security.

🖥 Device security
Security that comes built into your device.

💗 Device performance & health
Reports on the health of your device.

👪 Family options
Manage how your family uses their device.

Windows Desktops, Laptops and Tablets

Apps and Browser Control

The Windows Defender SmartScreen protects your device from apps and files downloaded from the Web, which may contain malware or phishing software.

Smartscreen also checks for malicious websites and the Web content used by apps in the Microsoft Store.

The **App & browser control** feature listed on pages 147 and 134 allows you to set SmartScreen to **Block** suspicious apps, files and websites or **Warn** you of dangers. You can also switch the SmartScreen Off, but this is obviously very risky.

Check apps and files

Windows Defender SmartScreen helps to protect your device by checking for unrecognised apps and files from the web.

○ Block

◉ Warn

○ Off

Device Security

This feature, shown on pages 147 and 134 is software built into your device which uses a **Secure boot** to protect your computer when it starts up. A piece of malware called a *rootkit* can bypass your log-ins, and record your passwords and keystrokes and other malicious activities.

⏻ Secure boot

Secure boot is on, preventing malicious software from loading when your device starts up.

Device Performance and Health

This **Protection Area**, listed on pages 147 and 134, highlights any problems such as lack of storage space and issues with apps and other software such as *device drivers*. A device driver is software which enables a piece of hardware such as a printer to work with your computer.

♡ Device performance & health

Check that your Windows is up-to-date and if there are any issues impacting your device health. The Health report shows the status of the most recent scan.

Fresh start: Use with Caution!

This feature, within **Device performance and health**, shown below, is intended to improve your device by removing your version of Windows 10 and installing the latest version, if necessary. Your personal files are kept but some apps may be deleted. If needed again, these apps will have to be re-installed.

Before using **Fresh Start** you should make a backup of all your important data.

♤ Fresh start

Start afresh with a clean and up-to-date installation of Windows.

Fresh start is a powerful procedure and should only be used if you are confident of restoring your apps and data files. Otherwise, for safety, the work should be entrusted to someone with more experience.

Windows Desktops, Laptops and Tablets

Family Options

This is a **Protection area** shown on pages 147 and 134. Amongst other things, **Family options** allows parents and grandparents, etc., to ensure that children make safe use of computers, without damaging their health or their parents' or grandparents' finances. These safeguards include:

- Putting money in children's Microsoft accounts, but setting limits, rather than letting them use your cedit card.

- Blocking unsuitable apps, games and websites.

- Limiting the time children spend on computers. (Addiction to video games is currently a serious problem with some children in the UK.**)**

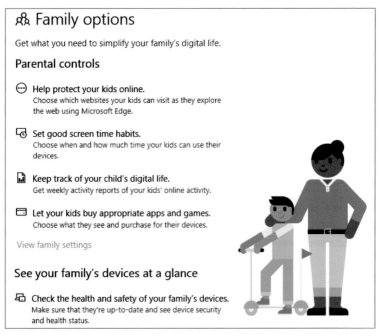

Windows Desktops, Laptops and Tablets

Windows Updates

As mentioned on page 132, major security problems have been caused in large organisations by not updating computers to the latest version of Windows. At the time of writing the latest version is Windows 10, but within Windows 10 there have been several security updates.

Windows 10 checks for updates and automatically downloads and installs them. Sometimes an update may fail to be installed. You can check for updates as discussed on pages 132 and 133. All being well you will see the following in **Start > Settings > Update & Security**.

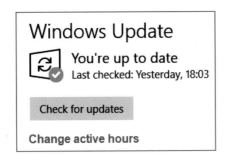

Alternatively you can select **Check for updates** shown above and you will see any updates available.

Windows Update

Updates are available.

- Windows Malicious Software Removal Tool

- 2018-06 Update for Windows 10 Version 1511

- Feature update to Windows 10, version 1803.

Windows Desktops, Laptops and Tablets

Windows Updates (Continued)

Active Hours

Although updates to Windows 10 may be installed automatically, **Change active hours** shown on the previous page allows you to set the times when you don't want the the updates to be installed. Also, updates will not be installed if you're currently using the computer.

Versions of Windows 10

Version 1703	Creators Update	May 2017
Version 1709	Fall Creators Update	October 2017
Version 1803	April 2018 Update	April 2018

Checking Your Version of Windows 10

- Select the **Start** button and the **Settings** gear icon shown on the right to open **Windows Settings**.

- Select **System** shown below.

- Select **About** at the bottom left of the screen to view information about your version of Windows 10, as shown in two Windows 10 machines below.

Windows specifications	
Edition	Windows 10 Pro
Version	1709
OS Build	16299.431

Windows specifications	
Edition	Windows 10 Home
Version	1803
Installed on	20/05/2018

Malware Protection

Introduction

Malicious software, or *Malware* for short, is software designed to invade your computer, steal your information or money or cause damage and inconvenience.

Microsoft Windows has its own Windows Defender security software to detect and eradicate malware, as discussed in Chapter 10. There are also many third-party companies producing security software, including Symantec (Norton), McAfee and Kaspersky. A single package may provide protection for several devices including smartphones, tablets and PCs, as shown below.

If you install a third party package such as Norton Security, it replaces the Microsoft Windows Defender security software features such as anti-virus and the firewall, etc.

Types of Malware

There are several types of malware, including *viruses*, *worms*, *Trojan horses*, *adware*, *spyware*, *ransomware* and *spam*. Writers of malware have been jailed after causing great disruption and financial damage worldwide.

Virus

The virus enters a computer system stealthily, often from a piece of software downloaded from the Internet or sent in an e-mail attachment. If not detected the virus multiplies and spreads throughout a hard disc or SSD (Solid State Drive) deleting saved files before infecting other computers. Some viruses may only cause trivial damage – such as displaying a "humorous" message – while others can corrupt software and paralyse a computer. Viruses can also be used to steal money and information. All smartphones, tablets and larger computers should have *anti-virus software* installed, as discussed shortly.

Worm

A worm is a computer program which exploits security weaknesses in networks such as the Internet, replicating itself from machine to machine. Worms can steal data, delete files and cause networks to slow down.

A worm called Mydoom was estimated to have infected a quarter of a million computers in a single day in 2004. This worm can open a "backdoor" which gives access to a computer, enabling the hacker to steal data.

Trojan Horse

The Trojan Horse, like the Wooden Horse of Troy, has an apparently genuine function, but it's really a piece of malware with criminal intent. It is not a virus since it does not replicate itself.

One such Trojan takes over a user's e-mail account and sends offensive messages – damaging the reputation of the innocent user. Logic Bombs and Time Bombs are Trojans triggered when a certain event or date occurs, such as Friday 13th.

BackDoor is a Trojan which connects to a victim's computer across the Internet, causing damage such as deleting files and generally wreaking havoc. Some Back Door Trojans can take over complete control of a computer.

Adware

This is software that displays pop-up advertisements on websites. These can be very annoying when they interrupt what you're doing. Some adware is not particularly dangerous — its purpose is to provide income for the advertisers and the websites. Some providers allow free use of their website but you have to tolerate the adverts. Otherwise you can pay a subscription to use the same site but without the advertisements.

However, some adware is dangerous and contains *spyware*, discussed on the next page. This is malware used to collect information from your computer, tablet or smartphone, etc., and pass it on to someone else.

Spyware

This type of malware can attack your device from within a piece of adware or from within a Trojan Horse or a *tracking cookie*, discussed on page 26. The spyware is software covertly installed on your computer or mobile device which transmits your information secretly to the attacker. This information can include your passwords, PIN and credit card numbers, your key strokes, websites visited and your e-mail contacts.

Spyware can use up a lot of a computer's resources, make it run slowly, cause it to crash and even overheat and sustain permanent damage.

Ransomware

This type of malware may be delivered in an innocent looking e-mail, but once installed can take over your computer or mobile device. Ransomware uses *encryption* to scramble your data so that you can no longer use it. A ransom is demanded by the attacker for the *key* (held by the attacker) to *decrypt* or unscramble the data so that you can use it again. The payment must be made using *Bitcoin digital currency* so that the attacker cannot be traced.

Other variations on the ransomware scam include the attacker pretending to be the police and imposing a fine, after accusing the victim of having illegal material saved on their hard drive, etc. Another scam is to threaten to broadcast on socal networking, etc., sensitive, personal and private information, discovered by the attacker on the victim's computer or mobile device, etc. Again the payment is demanded in Bitcoin.

Spam

This refers to the sending of very large numbers of unsolicited and unwanted e-mails, often originating from a *botnet*, as discussed below. Spam may be used for advertising or more sinisterly for *phishing*.

Phishing e-mails include a link to a fake website containing malware which may steal your passwords, bank details or other personal information. These phishing e-mails often pretend to be from your bank or large, well-known organisations such as Amazon or PayPal.

Botnet

Short for *Robot Network*, this means the connection of a large number of computers. The technology was originally used for the legitimate text communication system known as *Internet Relay Chat*. However, cyber criminals have hijacked the botnet technology for the execution of fraud and scams on a massive scale.

The criminals search the Web for computers and mobile devices with weak security and infect them with malware. The infected computers, known as *bots*, are then under the control of the cyber criminal's computer. The genuine users of bots may not notice that their devices have been infected.

A cyber criminal will seek to control thousands or even millions of bots and use their power to carry out crimes such as sending out millions of spam e-mails or a *DDoS* (*Distributed Denial of Service*). This is an attack intended to shut down computers, networks and websites.

Third party security software giving protection against malware in general is discussed in the rest of this chapter.

Security Software

The next few pages look at the Norton Security software package from the Symantec Corporation. This is just one example and there are many other similar products from reputable companies such as McAfee, Kaspersky and AVG.

The **BASIC** edition of Norton Security covers 1 PC and the **STANDARD** edition covers 1 PC or Mac. The **DELUXE** and **PREMIUM** editions can protect up to 5 or 10 devices respectively and are compatible with all the main types of computer, tablets and smartphones running the Windows, Android, and iOS (iPhone and iPad) operating systems.

If you have a mixture of devices such as a PC, tablet and smartphone, Norton Security Deluxe can be installed on all of your machines for a single yearly subscription.

The Norton Security Deluxe edition also includes the *Norton WiFi Privacy VPN* (Virtual Private Network) shown above. This is designed to keep you safe when using an insecure, free Wi-Fi Public Network, as mentioned on page 147 and discussed in more detail on page 166.

Features of Norton Security

- Norton Security automatically scans your device for viruses, spyware, Trojan horses, phishing and other malware and removes them. You can also start a manual scan at any time.

- *Automatic LiveUpdate* ensures that Norton Security can protect you from the latest viruses and malware.

- Norton Security includes a *two-way firewall* to prevent malware from *entering* your device.

- The firewall also monitors the flow of traffic *leaving* a computer. As mentioned earlier, cyber criminals can take control of lots of computers and use them to send out spam e-mails or viruses.

- Norton Security safeguards your identity, personal information and online transactions.

- The **Settings** screen shown below lists some of the main features in Norton Security.

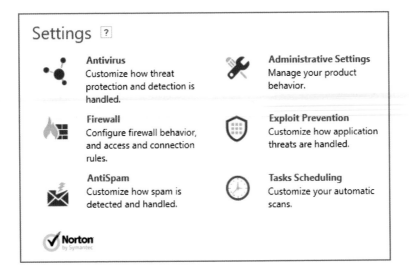

Settings ?

Antivirus
Customize how threat protection and detection is handled.

Administrative Settings
Manage your product behavior.

Firewall
Configure firewall behavior, and access and connection rules.

Exploit Prevention
Customize how application threats are handled.

AntiSpam
Customize how spam is detected and handled.

Tasks Scheduling
Customize your automatic scans.

Norton
by Symantec

Installing Norton Security

- You can buy Norton Security online and download it from **www.norton.com**.

- Alternatively you can buy a card containing instructions and a *Product Key* from a retail outlet, either online or from a High Street shop.

- Choose whether you want to buy a year's subscription for 1, 5 or 10 devices, i.e. smartphones, tablets and other computers.

- If you buy Norton Security online, you will need to create a Norton account with an e-mail address and password. After paying the subscription you will receive the Product Key by a confirmation e-mail.

Installing from the Norton Website

- In a Web browser such as Google Chrome, visit **www.norton/setup**. You may need to set up a Norton account with an e-mail address and password.

- Enter the 25-digit Product Key.

- You can then either **Agree and Continue** or **Skip Automatic Renewal** of your annual subscription.

- Select **Agree & Download** shown below to install Norton Security on the device you are currently using.

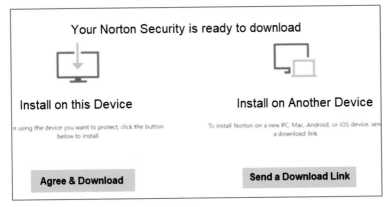

- Select **Run** and then **Download** (which takes about 10 minutes).
- Select **Yes** to allow Norton to make changes and then select **Agree & Install**.
- After the installation on a PC computer you should see the screen shown below. This reports the protection status of your device and allows you to carry out a **Quick Scan** for malware.

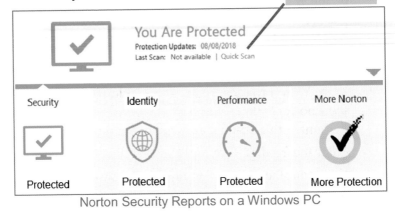

Norton Security Reports on a Windows PC

Installing on Other Devices

- If you bought a **DELUXE** or **PREMIUM** edition of Norton Security for 5 or 10 devices, select **Send a Download Link** shown on page 161. This opens the following window.

To extend your Norton protection, send a download link

PC   Mac   Android   iOS

To install Norton on another device, enter an email address below

myemail@mydomain.com

- Enter your e-mail address as shown above then click or tap the arrow. This sends a **Download Link** to your e-mail address.

- On another device, which can be a PC, Mac, Android or iOS, iPhone or iPad, open the e-mail from **Your Norton Team** .

- Select **Download Now** then follow the instructions.

- Select **Agree & Download** and **Agree & Install**.

PC Devices

- On PC machines continue as described on page 161.

Android and iOS Devices

- On Android and Apple iOS devices, after selecting **Download Now**, follow the instructions on the screen to install Norton Mobile Security app from the Google Play Store or the Apple App Store.

Android and iOS Devices (Continued)

Instead of using the **Install on Another** device option discussed on pages 161 and 162, you can also install Norton Mobile Security direct from the appropriate app store. You will need your Norton product key.

- Open the Google Play Store or the Apple App Store.

- Search for Norton Security and Antivirus (Android) or Norton Mobile Security (iPad and iPhone).

- Download and install the app.

- Open the app.

- If necessary, create a Norton e-mail address and password and sign in.

- Enter the Norton Product Key to activate the software.

- At the end of the installation you can select **Start Tour** to view the main features of Norton Security or **Skip Tour** to start using the software straightaway.

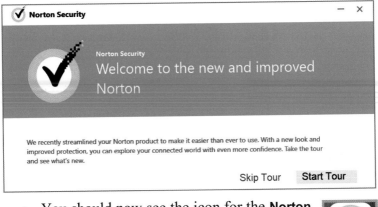

- You should now see the icon for the **Norton Mobile** app on your Home screen. Tap this to check your security at any time.

Android Devices

Norton Mobile Security on an Android device allows you to check several aspects of your security, as shown below.

Android Protection Features

Tap on a protection topic such as **Anti-Malware** or **Wi-Fi Security** above to view security reports as shown below.

Norton Security Reports on an Android Device

iPhones and iPads

When you tap the **Norton Mobile** icon shown on the right, the following screen appears.

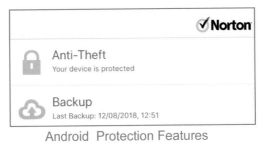

Android Protection Features

Compared with the **Norton Mobile Security** screen shown on page 164, most of the security features such as **Anti-Malware**, **Privacy** and **Wi-Fi Security** are absent. This is because the iOS operating system used on iPhones and iPads is generally regarded as much more secure than the Android operating system. Some of the reasons for this are:

- The Android operating system is *open-source*, so it's easier to write malware for Android. This contrasts with the very tightly controlled iOS operating system.

- iOS apps and their data are said to be *sandboxed*, i.e. isolated from other apps, so they can't share data, delete data or spread viruses to other apps.

- Apple keeps very tight control over apps entering the App Store, preventing the spread of malware.

So it may be argued that, currently, iPhones and iPads don't need the **Anti-Malware** and other security software shown on the previous page for Androids. The **Anti-Theft** feature in Norton Mobile shown above is similar to the iOS **Find iPhone** discussed on page 128. The **Backup** feature shown above is used to make copies of Contacts.

Virtual Private Networks (VPN)

At the time of writing, Norton Security Deluxe includes *Norton WiFi Privacy VPN*, as shown on page 158.

Norton WiFi Privacy

Secure private information like your passwords, bank details and credit card numbers when using public Wi-Fi on your PC, Mac or mobile device.

Public Wi-Fi networks in airports, cafés, etc., are easy targets for hackers to steal your data such as bank details.

To combat this there are many *Virtual Private Networks* used by large organisations and individuals alike, accessible to smartphones, tablets and PCs.

- The VPN is a secure, private network between your connection to a public network and the Internet.

- You connect to the VPN server using a *VPN client app* provided by a VPN provider such as Norton.

- The connection is made via an *encrypted tunnel* to the VPN server, so hackers can't access your data.

- After the VPN server you are *anonymous* on your journey to and from your Internet destination. Your IP (Internet Protocol) address which identifies your device on the Internet, your geographical location and your browsing activities are hidden from hackers.

- Beyond the VPN server you take on the identity (IP address and location) of the VPN server.

- Apart from **Norton WiFi Privacy**, there are many free VPN apps downloadable from Internet, the Google Play Store and the Apple App Store.

Setting Up a Mobile Hotspot

A smartphone can be used to connect Wi-Fi only tablets or laptops to the Internet in places where there is no Wi-Fi. As it's protected by a password this should be more secure than free public Wi-Fi. The phone becomes a *mobile hotspot* and acts like a Wi-Fi router in the home or office.

Setting Up an Android Phone as a Mobile Hotspot

- Make sure **Mobile data** is switched on in:

    Settings > Data usage > Mobile data

- From the **Settings** menu, select **More** then **Tethering & mobile hotspot**. Switch on **Mobile Wi-Fi hotspot**, then tap **Set up Wi-Fi hotspot** shown below.

- Enter a **Password** for the hotspot, as shown below and tap **SAVE**.

Setting Up an iPhone as a Mobile Hotspot

- Select **Settings** then **Mobile Data**.
- Tap **Personal Hotspot** and switch **Personal Hotspot** On.
- If necessary switch **Wi-Fi** or **Bluetooth** On.
- Tap **Wi-Fi Password** and enter a password.

Connecting a Tablet or Laptop to a Mobile Hotspot

- A Wi-Fi only tablet or laptop can be *tethered* to the mobile hotspot (Android or iPhone) by Wi-Fi, Bluetooth or by a USB cable.
- Tap the Wi-Fi icon on your tablet, laptop, etc.
- Select your smartphone from the list of available networks on the tablet, laptop, etc., as shown below for my **Moto G (5)** phone.

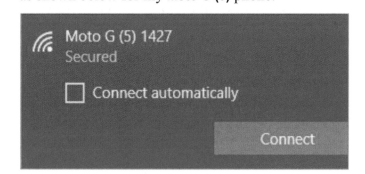

- Select **Connect** on the tablet, laptop, etc., to start using the Internet via your smartphone which is now acting as a Wi-Fi router.

> Using your phone as a mobile hotspot should be more secure than free public Wi-Fi. The data travels over a 3G/4G cell phone network and is *encrypted*. The mobile hotspot is also protected by your password.

Managing Your Data

Introduction

A *file* saved on your hard drive or SSD (Solid State Drive) may be a report, photo, or set of accounts, for example. Some files may be extremely valuable and irreplaceable, such as photos of once-in-a-lifetime family events or the memoirs or novel you've spent a year typing.

Apart from cybercrime attacks by *malware*, discussed earlier, data may be lost for some more innocent reasons:

- It is not unusual for a hard drive to fail, making the data inaccessible. This is less likely with an SSD.
- It's easy to delete the wrong file accidentally.
- If you save a file with the same name as an existing file, the earlier file is overwritten and lost.
- A power failure may cause you to lose a document or data you're working on.
- A mobile device can be lost or stolen very easily.
- You accidentally spill coffee over a computer or drop a mobile device into water.
- A computer may overheat or be damaged in a fire or flood.

Windows 10 keeps deleted files in a **Recycle Bin** with an icon on the Desktop from where they are recoverable for up to 90 days.

Android and iOS (iPhone and iPad) don't have their own recycle bin but third party apps are available.

Backup Files

It's essential to make regular backup copies of important files on removable media or in the Clouds on the Internet.

Backup copies should be stored in a different room or preferably a different building. Files backed up to the Clouds on the Internet are stored on *Web server* computers, most probably many miles away from your location.

Removable Media

Popular backup media include CDs, DVD, the *flash drive* or *USB memory stick* and the external hard drive.

Backing Up to the Clouds

The Clouds are really powerful server computers all round the world on the Internet. Major companies such as Microsoft, Google and Apple allow you to back up your data to servers located in the UK.

Popular Cloud storage systems which can be used to safely back up your data are Microsoft OneDrive, Google Drive (or simply Drive) and Dropbox. These systems can all be accessed on smartphones, tablets and computers in general, using the Windows, Android and iOS operating systems.

Cloud storage systems give free, extra storage space such as OneDrive (5GB), Google Drive (15GB) and Dropbox (2GB) with more available for a fee, e.g. by a monthly subscription.

OneDrive   Drive   Dropbox

The Cloud Backup Process

The main features of Cloud computing are:

- Files and photos saved on one device are *synced* or *uploaded* to the Clouds.

- The files and photos are then accessible *from the Clouds* <u>using any computer or mobile device</u> connected to the Internet, on which you are signed in with your account for OneDrive, Google Drive, etc.

- Depending on the settings, files and photos may be *automatically downloaded* from the Clouds and saved on the *local storage* on your other devices.

- If a file is modified, *sync* or *synchronisation* ensures all of your devices access the same, latest version.

Some advantages of Cloud storage are:

- The backup servers are managed by companies such as Microsoft, Google and Apple and therefore should be very secure.

- If your main machine suffers a failure, you can sign into another computer and use the backup copies from the Clouds or local storage.

- The Cloud servers will not be affected by any fire or flood which damages your computer, etc.

One possible disadvantage of Cloud storage:

Depending on your settings, if you *delete* a file from the local storage of one machine, it may be removed from your Cloud storage on the Internet and from the local storage *on all of your other devices*.

Installing Cloud Storage Apps

OneDrive, Google Drive, (also known as Drive) and iCloud/iCloud Drive are used here as examples, although there are other trustworthy and reliable storage systems.

Whichever storage system you use, you will need to create (or already know) your *user ID* for Microsoft (OneDrive), or Google (Google Drive), or Apple (iCloud/iCloud Drive), etc. This will consist of an e-mail address and password.

(iCloud is a straightforward Cloud storage system for Apple iOS devices. iCloud Drive includes *syncing*.)

Windows PC

- The general method is to download and install the app for OneDrive, Google Drive or iCloud/iCloud Drive from the Microsoft, Google or Apple websites. (OneDrive is pre-installed on Windows 8.1 and Windows 10).

- This places a listing for the app, such as **OneDrive**, in the Windows Start menu.

- **OneDrive** also appears on the Taskbar at the bottom right of the screen as shown below.

Windows creates two folders each for OneDrive, Google Drive and Dropbox etc., in the Windows File Explorer, as shown on the next page.

Internet or Cloud Folders

One folder, such as **Dropbox** in the **Quick access** area near the top left of the File Explorer, lists the files stored in the Clouds on the Internet. Also shown on the right, are **Google Drive** and **iCloud Drive**. A similar folder is created for **OneDrive**.

Local Folders

The second folder for each Cloud storage system holds duplicate copies of the files, but saved on the local storage on the device itself.

These folders are buried in the lower left of the File Explorer, within the folders on the hard drive, such as **iCloud Drive** shown below. These have a *pathname* such as:

This PC > OS (C:) > Users > Jill > iCloud Drive

OS(C:) above is the hard drive, **Users** is a *folder* and **Jill** and **iCloud Drive** are or *sub-folders* in the File Explorer.

Uploading Files to the Clouds: Windows PCs

You can save a document or photo in the clouds by opening it in the relevant app such as Word, Publisher, Photos, etc., then using **Save As** to browse to the folder for say, OneDrive or Google Drive, Dropbox or iCloud Drive, etc.

Or you can display the file in the File Explorer and *drag and drop* or *cut and paste* the file into the Clouds folder.

Android and iOS (iPhones and iPads)

OneDrive, Dropbox and Google Drive Cloud storage systems are available as apps from the Google Play Store and Apple App Store. iCloud Drive is available for iOS devices but is not yet easily available for Androids, although there are some third party solutions to install it.

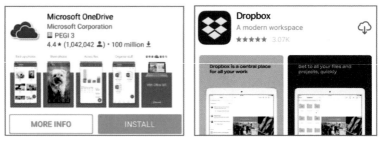

OneDrive in the Play Store   Dropbox in the App Store

The apps can be freely downloaded and installed from the Google Play Store or the Apple App Store.

After you've downloaded and installed a Cloud storage app, its icon should appear on the Home screen of your phone or tablet, as shown on page 170.

Uploading a File to the Clouds

- Open the file such as a photo in the Photos app on Android or iOS.

- Tap the photo or file to display the Android or iOS sharing or uploading icons shown below.

Android   iOS

- Select from a list of destinations for the file, including the **OneDrive, Google Drive** and **Dropbox Cloud** storage systems shown highlighted in red below.

- After selecting the Cloud storage system such as **OneDrive**, tap **Files** and select a **OneDrive** folder in which to store the file or photo, etc.

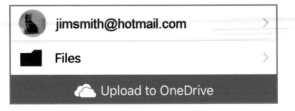

- Select **Upload to Onedrive** shown above to send the file to the Clouds. The file will now be available on any device you can sign into with an account for OneDrive.

Automatic Backups

Android Personal Data

- To make regular backups of all your personal data select **Settings > Backup & reset** and make sure **Back up my data** and **Automatic restore** are switched **On**. Also check that your **Backup account** is correct.

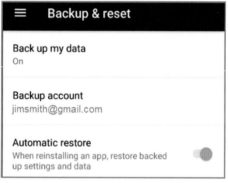

Android Photos

- Select the **Photos** app and from the 3-bar menu button select **Settings** and make sure **Back up & Sync** is **On** as shown below. This will share your photos to all the devices which have your Google Account set up.

Automatic Backups

iPhone and iPads

- Select the **Settings** icon shown on the right then tap your name near the top left and select **iCloud**.

- Scroll down and select **iCloud Backup** and make sure **iCloud Backup** is switched **On** with the green button as shown below.

❮ iCloud   **Backup**

BACKUP

iCloud Backup

Automatically back up data such as your accounts, documents, Home configuration and settings when this iPad is connected to power, locked and on Wi-Fi. Learn more...

Back Up Now

Last successful backup: 9 August 2018 at 08:14

Restoring Data: Caution Needed!

It's essential to keep backup copies of your data, but restoring it using **General > Reset** after a disaster involves the **Erase All Content and Settings** operation shown below. It may be advisable to seek help from an experienced friend or Apple Service Centre for this risky task.

❮ General   **Reset**

Reset All Settings

Erase All Content and Settings

Automatic Backups

Windows PC

- The **File History** feature shown below copies files from a PC to an external hard drive or a flash drive.

- Connect an external drive and select the Windows **Start** icon followed by the **Settings** icon shown on the right. Select **Update & security** and then **Backup**.

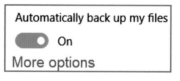

- Select **Add a drive** shown above. **File History** detects the drive. Select the drive and switch **Automatically back up my files** to **On**, shown below.

- **More options** shown above allows you to set the time between backups, such as every hour (default) and to select the folders under **Back up these folders**.

Using a PC to Back Up Mobile Devices

Smartphones and tablets can copy files to the Clouds as described earlier. If you have a PC, this can be used to access the files in the Clouds and then use **File History** to make extra, secure backups on an external hard drive or USB flash drive as described above.

Windows System Images

Desktops and laptops use hard drives spinning at high speed or SSDs (Solid State Drives) based on microchips, for the storage of software and data. Desktops and laptops may have 300GB to 1TB (1,000 GB) of storage while inexpensive Android phones or tablets, for example, may have as little as 8GB or 16GB. So the typical Windows laptop or desktop may be storing hundreds of important documents and irreplaceable photos. Sooner or later the hard drive or SSD may fail or be corrupted by malware.

The way to prevent this potential disaster is to create a *system image*. This is an exact copy of everything on a drive or on an independent section known as a *partition*.

The system image is copied to a removable storage device such as a USB external hard drive or SSD *with enough space to hold all of your device's software and data*. These are available in various sizes, up to 4TB — more than enough to copy a system image of a laptop or desktop PC.

If a hard drive or SSD fails, the system image can be restored to a new drive installed inside the computer.

Creating a System Image

- Plug the external drive into the PC and switch it on.
- Select the **Start** button shown on the right.
- Scroll down and select **Windows System** and then select **Control Panel**.
- In the **Control Panel** select **System and Security**.
- Select **Backup and Restore (Windows 7)**.

  (Please note: This also applies to Windows 10).

- Select **Create a system image** in the left-hand panel.

- In response to **Where do you want to save the backup?** select **On a hard disk**.
- Select **Start backup**.

The backup may take a few minutes or more than an hour. At the end of the backup you can opt to **Create a system repair disc** on a CD/DVD as shown below.

This can be used to boot up, i.e. start up your computer, if you had to install a new hard drive or SSD. Then restore the system image on the new drive as discussed below.

Restoring a System Image

- Connect the external drive holding the system image.
- Select the **Windows 10 Settings** gear icon.
- Select **Update & Security**.
- Select **Recovery > Advanced start-up > Restart now**. This restarts the PC.
- Select **Troubleshoot > Advanced options**.
- Select **System Image Recovery**.
- Enter your Windows password and select your system image to start the restoration process, which can take a few minutes or several hours.

Index